THE
COMPLETE BOOK OF
TAROT

THE
COMPLETE BOOK OF
TAROT

JULIET SHARMAN-BURKE

St. Martin's Press
New York

To Geoff, with love

Library of Congress Cataloging-in-Publication Data

Sharman-Burke, Juliet.
  The complete book of Tarot.

    1. Tarot.   I. Title.
BF1879.T2S53   1986   133.3'2424   86-1277
ISBN 0-312-15634-0
ISBN 0-312-00579-2 (pbk.)

First published in Great Britain by Pan Books Ltd.

Contents

ACKNOWLEDGEMENTS

Thanks to Rich Leigh for his invaluable encouragement with this book and over the years; to Deb Buxton for her help in compiling and typing the correspondence course out of which this book grew; to my father Gerald Burke for his help in editing and to Sandra Wastiage whose practical support was so much appreciated and who sadly did not live to see publication.

Foreword

This book is intended to give you a comprehensive understanding of the Tarot as well as encouraging as much as possible your own study and involvement in the learning process. Some of you may want to study the Tarot in order to interpret the cards for others; some may wish to use it as an aid in personal growth and development. I hope that most of you will wish to do both.

This book has developed out of many years of teaching Tarot in workshops and by correspondence, so my personal method and style have been reproduced here as much as possible. For instance, I have included 'guided fantasy' exercises because so many students have found them useful in both the memorizing process and in gaining a deeper personal knowledge of each card. Because reading the Tarot relies so heavily on the reader's intuitive and interpretative prowess it is not an easy subject to teach. However, I do not believe that any special clairvoyant or psychic powers are needed in order to become a sensitive reader. All of us have intuitive powers within us naturally and reading the Tarot is certainly one good way of heightening and developing these qualities. The exercises should stimulate the imagination and in turn the unconscious powers of intuition. I also found that the idea of the Fool's journey through the Tarot (see page 22), incorporating myths and legends, caught students' imagination because they felt able to relate it to their personal stages of growth. The message of each card touches on some aspect of everyone's life, and in learning it you take a fresh look at yourself.

The Tarot is made up of seventy-eight cards. The deck is divided into twenty-two Major Trumps and fifty-six Minor Arcana. The Major Arcana are easily distinguishable by their unusual names and images – Fool, Magician, Empress, etc. The remaining fifty-six cards are divided into four suits rather like our modern playing cards. They are named differently though: Wands, Cups, Swords and Pentacles, and unlike playing cards each suit has four Court cards consisting of King, Queen, Knight and Page. Many packs have no pictorial images on the Minor cards which makes them quite complicated to learn; however the

Rider-Waite pack, used for illustration here, has images on all the 'pip' cards which is extremely helpful for beginners.

I have divided the book into four sections, the first three of which explain the cards, and each section ends with some suggested exercises. The fourth section concentrates on interpretation and how to go about a reading. I have included a number of example readings I have done to illustrate possible style and interpretation. The book has been arranged in such a way as to interlink the learning process and the path of self-discovery. The Major and Minor cards are mixed together in each section to encourage equal interest in both; for what often seems to happen is that the twenty-two Major Trumps are learnt first, and as they can be used successfully on their own, the task of learning another fifty-six cards gets put off. This is a pity because the Minor cards are an extremely valuable addition to the Major Arcana, on which we will concentrate later at greater depth.

A number of authors have approached the Tarot from a psychological point of view, particularly drawing on the ideas of C.G. Jung. I have also followed this line, and, in order to make the Fool's story of psychological development easier to follow, I have slightly changed the numerical sequence of the Major Trumps, which in fact brings it nearer to the numbering of the earlier decks. There is much controversy over the numbering of the Major cards, and it would appear that the earliest packs were not numbered at all. Indeed, many were not even named – the card simply bore the pictorial image. The eighteenth-century occult revival was responsible for much of the rectified numbering (see page 12).

Another relatively modern innovation is reading a significance into reversed cards, which I personally don't do. Reversals can be more confusing and baffling than informative, for each Tarot card carries within its upright position both positive and negative possibilities. The surrounding cards ought to be enough to indicate the 'weight' of the card in the spread.

The cards are intended as springboards for the intuitive powers to start working from and feelings evoked by the images are therefore the final touchstone for good divinatory interpretation. The more you get to know your cards – using the guided fantasy exercises helps a great deal – the more your intuitive powers will be heightened, and the more sensitive a reader you will become. If you immerse yourself initially in the study of the cards themselves you will find it far quicker and easier to interpret readings intuitively. The more you sow, the more you will reap.

The origins of the cards

Almost as fascinating and mysterious as the Tarot cards themselves is their lack of proven origin. A great many authors have
written exhaustively about the subject and many have ridden
themselves saddle-sore on one or another of their pet hobby
horses; yet none have managed to prove conclusively from
whence the Tarot originates. Different writers have proposed
various geographical roots, including Spain, southern France, the
Far East and Egypt, and part of the Tarot's richness is that it has
elements in common with so many different countries' myths and
legends. However, a direct line of descent from any one area
remains impossible to establish. As A.E. Waite says in the preface
to *Tarot of the Bohemians*: 'The chief point regarding the history
of the Tarot cards, whether used as pretexts for fortune telling or
as symbols of philosophical interpretation, is that such history
does not in fact exist.'* Although Waite wrote this in the late
nineteenth century, his statement remains valid today. We are still
no nearer knowing for certain the origins of the Tarot, yet it is well
worth taking a look at some of the interesting theories that have
been put forward.

One theory suggests that Tarot originated in China, where
playing cards were definitely used before the eleventh century AD
but there is little other evidence to support this. Alternatively,
India is a possible birth-place, and it is feasible that the four suits
of the Minor Arcana could refer to the four castes of Hinduism:
the Cup to the priests or Brahmins, the Sword to the warriors or
Kshatriyas, the Coin to the merchants or Vaisyas, and the Rod to
the serfs or Sudras. The Major Arcana has possible links with
Buddhism: the Fool could be the wandering monk, whose path of
enlightenment parallels the path taken by the Tarot Fool.

The first documented appearance of the cards in Europe can
be traced to 1392 when a sum was entered in the court ledger of
King Charles VI of France. The entry stated that money had been
paid to a painter by the name of Jacquemin Gringonneur for three

*Gérard Encausse, 'Papus', *Le Tarot des Bohémiens* (Paris, 1889).

packs of cards illustrated in 'gold and diverse colours ornamented with many devices . . . '

In 1377 a certain Brother Johannes of Bredfeld, Switzerland, wrote an essay* in which he described a game of cards which outlined the state of the world as it was then, in terms of society's structure. He went on to say, however, that he was entirely ignorant of when it was invented, where, and by whom. He suggested that the cards portrayed kings, noblemen and commoners, and could therefore be used for moral purposes to map out a society and its structure, and to teach people the lesson of knowing and keeping to their place. Brother Johannes appears to have taken the suits to represent the classes of society: Cups for the churchmen, Swords for the aristocracy, Coins for the merchants and Wands for the peasants.

At the time Tarot first appeared in Europe, Christianity reigned more or less supreme. The Church was busy stamping out paganism and vanquishing unorthodox Christian sects such as the Waldenses, Cathari and Bogomils. The chivalric order of Knights Templar also fell from the Church's favour early in the fourteenth century, and the order was destroyed. However, a large number of doctrines preached by heretical sects survived and are today collectively known as gnosticism, meaning a belief in esoteric knowledge. Gnosticism often combined Indian, Chaldean, Persian and Egyptian magical doctrines with Greek philosophy, Hebrew cabalistic belief and teachings of early Christianity. It is from these gnostic cults that many Western esoteric arts have evolved, including, quite possibly, the Tarot. Ironically, many of the forbidden pagan cults and doctrines survived within the walls of the Church which was trying so hard to obliterate them: for the monasteries preserved documents on the old religions including conjuring and spell books. As the images on the Tarot cards are mainly pagan in origin, and the gods of the old religions become the devils of the new, the cards were sometimes referred to as the devil's books. It is probably for these reasons that many people even today fear the Tarot as being something evil or devilish, connected with black magic and witchcraft.

At the time of a revival in esoteric and occult interests in the eighteenth century, certain French occultists claimed that the Tarot originated in Egypt and contained the purest doctrines of

*Tilley, Roger, *Playing Cards* (Octopus Books, London, 1973).

the Egyptian priests, who were said to have concealed secrets in the images of the cards to protect and preserve them from the uninitiated. They thought the cards had been brought into Europe by the gypsies, who were then believed to have emigrated from Egypt. The pioneer in this school of thought was Antoine Court de Gebelin, a clergyman deeply interested in the secret lore and doctrines of ancient Egypt. This was a subject which enjoyed extremely fashionable attention at the time, along with all sorts of other esoteric and occult matters. Court de Gebelin thought the Tarot images of the Major Arcana were remnants of the Book of Thoth, and wrote a highly acclaimed book in which he connected the Major Arcana to the secret beliefs and traditions of ancient Egypt. He brought the Tarot overnight recognition and made its use and understanding essential to all 'true occultists'. The nine volume book was entitled *The Primitive World Analysed and Compared with the Modern World.†*

According to Gebelin, the ancient custom was to stand in the temples of Thoth, whose walls were adorned with pictorial images representing the major forces governing the patterns of life. The person wishing to consult the gods would throw a loose bundle of rods at random, and as they fell with varying emphasis toward one image or another, the priests would interpret the patterns which were known as 'the words of the gods'. Out of this custom grew the practice of carrying the images around in card form, 'the unbound leaves of the sacred book of Thoth Hermes Trismegistus'. In this way, consultation with the gods became much less complicated and any room could be turned into a 'temple' simply by producing the pack of cards.

In the nineteenth century, a French Rosicruician and cabalist, Eliphas Levi, stressed the apparent link between the twenty-two letters of the Hebrew alphabet and the twenty-two Major Arcana. The Major cards were renumbered to fit into this cabalistic system and many modern packs follow the numerical order of this time. The letters of the Hebrew alphabet were said to connect with the twenty-two paths of the cabalistic Tree of Life, which, among other things, illustrates how the world came into being through the ten divine emanations or spheres (corresponding to the Minor Arcana cards, Ace to Ten). Levi also connected the four suits with

---

*Court de Gebelin, Antoine, *Le Monde Primitif Analysé et Comparé avec le Monde Moderne* (Paris, 1781).

the letters forming the unpronounceable great name of God, JHVH: J-Wands-fire;   H-Cups-water;   V-Swords-air; H-Pentacles-earth. The connections between cabala and Tarot can be studied in greater detail in the books listed in the bibliography.

The Minor Arcana

It is not known whether the Major and Minor Arcana were created together, or whether each was a separate tradition and they simply joined forces along the way. The Minor cards are an often neglected, but very important part of the deck, and in readings they add detail and fullness to the deeper, psychologically significant Major cards. The Major Trumps give information and guidance on the seeker's inner life and psychological state. The Minor cards expand this with details of relationships, work, creative potentials, strife and success in a more specific way. The Major cards are said to be spiritual while the Minor are regarded as mundane, and the Court cards act as a bridge between the two.

Once again, the root of the Minor Arcana's symbolism could come from various quarters, some of which have already been touched on briefly. Another theory, put forward by Jessie Weston* is that the Tarot emblems, the Wand, the Cup, the Sword and the Pentacle, were connected with the four Grail Hallows or sacred objects found in the Grail castle of Arthurian legend. Miss Weston thought that such arcane wisdom was a secret of the fourteenth-century Knights Templar who were believed to be privy to the inner mystery of the Grail. The Tarot suits and the Grail Hallows couple thus:

WAND: The lance of Longinus, the Roman soldier said to have pierced Christ's side as He hung from the Cross.

CUP: The Grail itself, the cup used by Jesus at the Last Supper.

SWORD: King David's legendary sword of the spirit referred to in the Old Testament.

---

*Weston, Jessie, *From Ritual to Romance* (first pub. 1920) Anchor Books, New York, 1957).

PENTACLE: The plate from which the Last Supper was eaten.

The four Grail Hallows seem, in turn, to have descended from the Four Treasures of Ireland, the magical emblems of Celtic myth. These treasures of Ireland were said to have belonged to the pre-Christian Celtic gods known as the Tuatha de Danaan or the People of the Goddess Danu. The chieftains of the Tuatha were expected by their people to maintain well-being and prosperity of the land through their supernatural powers. The gods were aided in this by four magical treasures: the spear of Lug; the cauldron of The Dagda; the sword of Nuada and the Stone of Fal. These four treasures show striking similarities to the four Grail Hallows and the four Tarot suits.

WAND: The Spear of Lug, a supremely versatile god known to his people as 'many skilled'. Legend goes that when he arrived, wishing to join the Tuatha de Danaan, he was asked by the guard to state his craft. Lug replied carpenter, and was informed that the Tuatha already had a carpenter. Lug added that he was also a smith, only to be told they already had a smith too. Lug then claimed he was not only a carpenter and a smith, but also a warrior, a harpist, a historian, a poet, a sorcerer, a hero and many other things beside. Each post was reputedly filled, but when Lug demanded to know whether the court had a single member who possessed all these skills it seemed they had not, so Lug was triumphantly admitted to join the Tuatha de Danaan. When we come to look closely at the 'flavour' of each suit, we will see how admirably this tale fits with the suit of Wands and their element, fire.

CUP: The Cauldron of the Dagda, the All-Father, could never be emptied, and no-one left with his hunger unsatisfied. The Dagda was known as the nourisher of all his people and his inexhaustible cauldron was even able to bring the dead back to life. This treasure is connected with the Cups, and their element, water.

SWORD: The deadly sword of Nuada, King of the Tuatha, was so powerful that, when unsheathed, no enemy could ever escape it. The suit of Swords, associated with strife and battle, connects with this treasure, and the element, air, fits well as the element which seeks out the inescapable truth.

PENTACLE: The Stone of Fal, the coronation seat of Irish Kings, was said to cry out loud when sat upon by the rightful King of Ireland. The stone of Saint Columba, a cross-patterned stone found in old Celtic churchyards, seems to have connections with the Stone of Fal, which like the stone of Columba, was also found floating magically upon water. The Seige Perilous is the Arthurian equivalent of the chair in which only the true High Prince could be safely enthroned. This treasure combines the earthy, and yet magical, quality attributed to the Pentacles and their element, earth.

There is some further elaboration of the overall meanings of each suit in a reading, on page 45, when we come to study each card in depth.

As can be seen from these similarities the Tarot seems to combine, in a way too striking perhaps to be coincidental, Judeo-Christian symbols and mysterious Celtic images. The same combination of Celtic elements and Judeo-Christian motifs emerged in the Grail romances, those mysterious and poetic compilations which began to appear around 1180–1200, and took European culture by storm. All that can be said for certain is that the Tarot, like the Grail legends, reflects a synthesis of diverse currents of the thought and tradition prevalent in Europe at the time Tarot first appeared, and it is possible that there is a link between them yet to be explained by historians or scholars.

The Grail legends reflect a path of personal development and integration which make it clear they are not merely stories but are symbolic of the process of striving towards self-awareness and illumination. In about 1250, the church heavily condemned the Grail romances because of their pagan and heretical motifs. Although the idea is not proven, it may be that an explanation of the Tarot's existence is as a pictorial version of these legends, coded as a pack of cards in order to preserve them.

At the end of a somewhat fruitless attempt to find the Tarot's true origins, we can nevertheless take comfort in the fact that at least the cards have found their mysterious way to us.

How the Tarot works

The riddle of why the Tarot cards work lies within the mind of the reader rather than in the actual cards. The images act as mirrors which offer a reflection of unsuspected knowledge buried deep in the unconscious mind. Rachel Pollack* says that while ancient peoples spoke of the 'other worlds' or the 'land of the gods', today we speak of the 'unconscious'. She points out that the underlying experience remains: a realm of being in which time does not exist and knowledge is not limited to the images received from our senses. The Tarot works as a bridge between our conscious and unconscious knowledge. Answers and knowledge arise out of the unconscious through dream, fantasy and intuition, and the Tarot cards stimulate this intuition when sensitively read.

Paul Huson†, a modern Tarot authority, suggests that learning the meanings of the pictorial images on the cards can be compared with, or possibly even arose from, ancient 'memory systems' or 'ars memorativa'. The Greeks invented an art of memory system based on impressing a sequence of images with a particular significance upon the mind to improve memory recall. This method was passed on via the Romans, and was used a great deal by medieval monks. In those days, books were rare and costly, so student monks memorized lengthy tracts by heart from the few available books and manuscripts. To aid their memory of such large portions of information, they used pictures or specially arranged symbols around which to focus each section of the text. The material would be filed away, as it were, under the 'heading' of the particular image or picture, in the back of the scholar's mind. When a particular chapter or tract needed to be retrieved, the student would simply look at appropriate key images, and the knowledge would automatically come forward to his conscious mind. This system was used in memorizing religious creeds and the Stations of the Cross, still used in Catholic churches, is an example of this practice in use today.

*Pollack, Rachel, *Seventy-eight Degrees of Wisdom* (The Aquarian Press, Northamptonshire, 1983).
†Huson, Paul, *The Devil's Picturebook* (Abacus, London, 1971).

However, the monks did not include one special practice which had been a central part of classical memory systems. This was the 'enlivening' of the imagination, believed to bring additional mysterious benefits as well as an excellent memory. In many ways, learning to read the Tarot works in a similar way to 'ars memorativa'. Using the images on the cards to enrich and enliven the imagination, the reader gains a special insight into the cards and their meanings. By learning the symbols on each card in this way, the associations will spontaneously reveal themselves each time a card is laid out. The Tarot images act like mirrors, reflecting things that the unconscious mind already knows, and feeding this information through to the conscious mind. Those images are powerful archetypes which can identify relevant associations with unexpected accuracy if left to their own devices.

Getting to know your cards

Getting to know your Tarot deck is obviously a vital part of the initial process of understanding Tarot. Although the Rider-Waite pack is used to illustrate this book, you can certainly choose whichever pack you like best. The images should appeal to your sense of style and colour; for the pictures need to be impressive enough for you to turn them into effective 'mind mirrors'. The old superstition that to buy your own pack is unlucky can be safely ignored. After all, the most important thing is to feel at home with your cards; they should be like friends, intimate and familiar. There is a possibility this might not be achieved with a pack you have not selected yourself. There are several different styles to choose from: the 14th-century Visconti pack; the woodcut Marseilles deck; the more modern Morgan-Greer, or the ultra-modern 007 deck, and many more besides. It is well worth spending some time and trouble in deciding your preference because once you start working with one set of images it is difficult to switch to others.

Having made your choice, examine the images carefully: the exciting process of getting to know the cards is just beginning. Treat them with respect, treasure them as something very special to you alone, and try not to let other people handle them casually. Some readers keep cards in a little box; others wrap them in a cloth. I use the traditional black silk square which is supposed to keep the cards neutral and protect them from negative energies. Whichever method you choose, the importance lies in the care and effort you take in making and keeping a relationship with your cards. Many Tarot readers prepare for a reading by some method of relaxation such as a series of breathing exercises. The rhythm relaxes the body, and in turn the mind, so that the intuitive powers are free to come to the fore. It is helpful to work out, and stick to, a particular routine for the preliminaries to a reading which will help to distinguish it as your own individual style.

It is important to use imagination and fantasy to get to know your cards and interpret their images so that the intuitive levels of the unconscious are stirred. A good way of doing this is to make up stories about each card, letting your imagination revolve around the chosen image. If you do this several times you will find the card starts to produce its own associated images. Make a note of the images which recur. Acquiring this habit can increase your personal feeling about each card as you build your own rapport with the images. Let yourself really *feel* the heat of the blazing Sun; let the cool mist rising from the dewy pond on the Moon card send shivers down your spine; smell the fresh summer's scent in the Empress's cornfield; hear the loud blast from the Judgement's trumpet. This is all part of 'enlivening' your imagination. It may seem an effort, but if you are serious in your wish to become a good Tarot reader you cannot take short cuts. Once you get involved in the enchanted world of imagination and fantasy it will become too much fun to seem like work!

To develop yourself as a truly sensitive Tarot reader you have to be serious in your intention. You need to be aware of what your cards can and cannot do for you. They can give indications and guidelines for future events, they can clarify a difficult situation, which makes it possible for you to start thinking about it in a different light, and they can suggest opportunities for change or action. The energy of the cards seems to indicate the possibilities available, but you need to go halfway to meet them. Just as it is no good sitting inside when the sun is shining, hoping to get brown, the energies and opportunities indicated by the cards still have to be acted upon. If the cards suggest change, do something positive about it. If they suggest you do nothing, take heed, for the cards always give clear pointers. One client came for a reading to ask advice about complications which had arisen during a house purchase. The cards indicated it was not a good proposition, and that it would prove too much for him to cope with. However, the client took no notice and proceeded with the legal battles and finally bought the house, only to find that he could not manage the payments and was forced to sell almost immediately. He consulted me over the next purchase and on that occasion the cards were more favourable. As far as I know he is still in the second house.

Another common difficulty when beginning reading for friends, is pre-judging situations. This happened to me when I was first learning to read Tarot, when a friend asked me if she would ever marry. She had wanted to get married for a long time but had not done so, but I personally doubted that she ever would. When the cards indicated love, marriage and a change of residence, I was surprised, disbelieving and almost tempted not to tell her the good news in the cards in case it did not come true, so sure was I that I knew best. Nevertheless, I read the cards truthfully, and three days after the reading she met the man she married six months later and moved to another country. This is a prime example of how difficult it can be to suspend your own judgement; and yet it is a necessary lesson to learn.

However, what the cards will not do is state any definite, unchangeable events. Their message is often necessarily vague, for it is important to give your seeker room to make up his or her own mind about a matter. Specific questions are very difficult to answer, and the cards should be used as a guideline rather than a hard-and-fast way to behave. The Tarot cards make an excellent guide but a bad master. When dealing with difficult situations in a reading, try to see why the seeker is in whatever difficulties he or she is in. Try to discuss what can be done; sometimes just acknowledging the difficulties can help in itself. Often Tarot readers are consulted when their clients are in a state of confusion, indecision or difficulty, both mentally and emotionally. They will ask for help from the cards when they have a problem to solve, so be prepared to listen as well as to talk. I give some sample readings in the fourth part of the book to suggest how such problems can be tackled.

PART ONE

THE FOOL
THE MAGICIAN
THE EMPRESS
THE EMPEROR
THE HIGH PRIESTESS
THE HIEROPHANT
THE LOVERS
THE CHARIOT

THE ACES
THE TWOS
THE THREES
THE FOURS
THE FIVES

The Fool's Journey

I would like to treat the Major Trumps in terms of the Fool's journey through various stages of life, a familiar theme in a great many myths, legends and fairy tales. The Fool's story makes the Tarot easier to learn and understand, especially because this theme is, broadly speaking, that of everyone's life. The basic myth starts with the birth of a hero, often a person with mortal and divine parentage. In our story, the hero is The Fool and we follow his life through childhood and education (The Magician), meeting his mortal parents (The Empress and The Emperor) his divine parents (The High Priestess and The Hierophant) his loves and conflicts (The Lovers and The Chariot) and his worldly trials of adulthood (Justice, Temperance, Strength and The Hermit). Half-way through his life (The Wheel of Fortune) the Fool experiences some form of loss or crisis. This evokes in him a need to change (The Hanged Man, Death) and is followed by his journey into the underworld in order to discover what is responsible for this crisis, (The Devil, The Tower). After his struggles with darkness, he goes on to encounter the celestial bodies of The Star, The Moon and

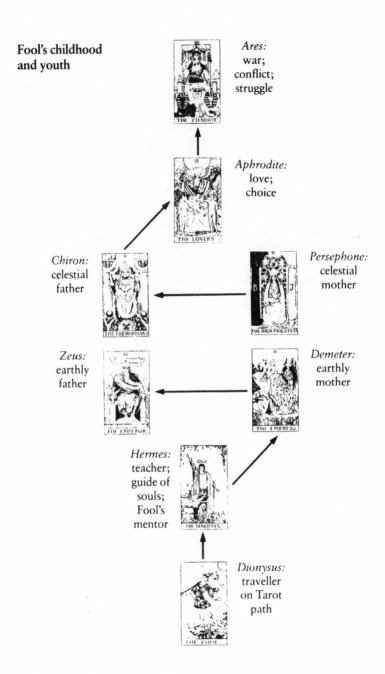

Fool's childhood and youth

Ares: war; conflict; struggle

Aphrodite: love; choice

Chiron: celestial father

Persephone: celestial mother

Zeus: earthly father

Demeter: earthly mother

Hermes: teacher; guide of souls; Fool's mentor

Dionysus: traveller on Tarot path

The Sun, and his victory over darkness results in rebirth (Judgement) and triumph (The World).

The Tarot images are archetypal, as is the story this journey tells, and some myths and legends overlap. As many mythological figures have much in common with specific cards, I have found it useful to associate each card with a particular mythical story or figure and, on the whole, I have stuck to Greek myths. This helps to provide a sense of the card, its meanings and its resonances. The myth of The Judgement of Paris, for example, adds a much richer dimension to the Lovers card than its bald key-word description 'a love affair with a trial or choice'.

The Tarot often uses imagery depicting the four elements: fire, water, air and earth, which feature so prominently in astrology, alchemy and the whole spectrum of esoteric thought. Some, though not all, of the cards can be associated with zodiac signs or their planets, and, when appropriate, I have included them.

Let us now look at the cards in detail, starting with The Fool.

THE FOOL

The image of the Fool starts off the Major Arcana sequence. In many ways he is the most important card in the pack. The Fool is the only one of the Major Arcana to live on in the modern playing deck, where he exists as the Joker. The Joker in modern games is known as a 'wild' card, one who can take the place of any other card and, like the Tarot Fool, is unnumbered and can mean all or nothing.

Let us take time to examine the imagery in depth. The central figure is of a gaily dressed youth, whose open arms almost seem to embrace the world. He shoulders a staff with a bag attached to it, and holds up high a single white rose. His upturned face and posture suggest energy and adventure. A small dog leaps excitedly at his ankle as together they prepare to step off the edge of the imposing precipice. This is the first step of the Fool's journey into the unknown; yet his expression is calm and confident. The cliff edge is forefront, so we cannot see what lies beneath the Fool; and the Fool himself does not even look. Behind him, in the distance, rear icy mountain peaks, jagged and snow-clad. The mountains appear hard and uninviting, difficult terrain to travel along, but the valley beneath appears flatter, greener and more welcoming. A bright sun fills the right hand corner of the card and the sky is cloudless.

The Fool carries his staff and bundle lightly; it does not appear to be a heavy burden. The bundle represents the past experiences of which he has no immediate need. The staff is black, the colour of power and energy, although in the Fool's case it is as yet untapped. If we look very closely we can make out that the clasp on the bag is in the form of an eagle's head. This suggests the spirit, perhaps the flight into the unknown. The eagle is the sacred bird of Zeus, the Greek All-Father, who has important connections with the Fool, as we shall see. There is intricate detail on the Fool's hat too. It is made up of interwoven laurel leaves, a symbol of success, and adorned with a red feather, the colour of desire, perched jauntily on top. Interestingly, the same laurel leaves crown the dancing figure on the World, which is the final card in the Major Arcana. The Fool wears multi-coloured clothing, reflecting the muddled impulses within him which pull in different directions. His dog symbolizes the instinctive fear which all men share of the unknown, while his step off the edge of the precipice shows that, despite his fear, he is prepared to take the plunge into uncharted terrain.

In this Tarot tale, the Fool is our hero. The figure of the Fool could be associated with a number of Greek, Egyptian or Celtic heroes, many of whom have a similar story. Born of both mortal and divine parents, the hero follows a quest which involves him in facing many different situations including conquering the forces of darkness before achieving his goal in triumph. Dionysus is a Greek god whose character has much in common with the Tarot Fool. Dionysus, the god of free spirit, was known as an overturner of hidebound traditions and restrictions. He was the god of madness as well as ecstasy. One myth tells that Dionysus was born of the union of Zeus and Semele, a mortal. However, when Zeus's jealous wife Hera discovered that Semele was carrying her husband's child, she disguised herself as the girl's maid and persuaded Semele to insist that Zeus reveal himself to her in his divine

THE FOOL.

glory. When he did so she was immediately scorched to death by a brilliance too great for mortal flesh to behold. Nevertheless, Zeus managed to save the unborn Dionysus and sealed the foetus in his thigh until it was ready to be delivered. When the baby Dionysus was finally born, Zeus entrusted him to Hermes' care and upbringing. Another Orphic version of the birth of Dionysus tells that he was born of Zeus and Demeter, the earth mother, and that the Titans, older gods jealous of Dionysus's noble birth, tore him limb from limb and boiled him in a cauldron. Zeus however stepped in again, saving the child's heart which he fed to Persephone, queen of the underworld, in the form of pomegranate seeds. Persephone gave birth to Dionysus-Zagreus, god of light and ecstasy. The chief characteristic in common with the Tarot Fool is the conquering of death and triumphant rebirth.

The Fool is like each of us on our various quests through life. He is like the child discovering life for the first time, or the adult searching for a new meaning or sense of purpose. The Fool seeks the truth, and turns his attention towards the spirit in search of truth. His madness or foolishness links him to the divine, for originally the word 'silly' meant 'blessed'. The Fool is simple, trusting, innocent and ignorant of the trials and pitfalls that await him, yet he is prepared to abandon his old ways and take the leap into the unknown.

Perhaps you can identify with the Fool as you start a new adventure and prepare to journey with him through the Tarot. Like the Fool you are moving into unfamiliar territory, not knowing where it may lead you. Learn with him as he travels the various paths of knowledge, development and self-awareness.

When the Fool appears in a reading, you may be sure that an unexpected influence will soon come into play. There may be a sudden unlooked for opportunity, or the possibility of an adventure or escape. The Fool represents the need to abandon the old ways and start something new and untested. Anything could happen, so hold your nose and jump!

THE MAGICIAN

The Magician is the first person the Fool encounters on his journey through life. The image on the card shows a young black-haired man dressed in a white robe and scarlet cloak. His belt depicts a snake eating its own tail. The Magician holds one hand up, and the other points down; before him on a table stand four objects: a wand, a cup, a sword and a pentacle. At the foot of the card is a rich garden filled with flourishing lilies and roses. The Magician wears white, to signify his inner purity, and red to symbolize his purposeful activity. His belt is the symbol of eternity and the figure eight above his head stands for infinity. He holds a white wand heavenwards symbolising the purity of his higher aspirations. He points up to the heavens and down to the earth, for he is a link between the gods and men, spirit and matter.

The objects before him correspond with the four suits of the Minor Arcana, and also with the four elements which in ancient times were thought to form the world: fire, water, air and earth. They can also correspond with the Jungian four functions of consciousness: intuition, feeling, thinking and sensation. Already, in this first stage of the journey, is contained the seed of the various experiences the Fool will encounter in the cards to come.

The Magician is often compared with Hermes, the Greek messenger god. Hermes was an extremely versatile god. Not only did he carry messages between gods and men: he also acted as protector on all journeys even in his sombre role of psychopomp or guide of souls of the dead to the underworld. He was the god of the mind and education, as well as commerce, including wheeling-dealing. He was also a trickster, loving to play mischievous pranks on gods and men alike, but was always popular with both on account of his good nature. He was entrusted with the care of young Dionysus, in the same way that the Magician takes care of the Fool.

The four items on the Magician's table link up with the attributes of Hermes: the wand with the caduceus, his herald's staff of office which all respected; the sword with that given to him by Zeus with which to slay Argos, the many-eyed monster;

the cup with the cup of fortune which Hermes gave mortals to drink from in order to change their fortune, either for joy or sorrow; and the pentacle with the coin symbolizing his guise as protector of merchants and thieves. All manner of divination came under Hermes's jurisdiction, including the ancient methods of using each or all of the four elements to foretell the future. Hermes was granted the powers of divination by Apollo, and these powers of divination and transformation have earned him the title Lord of the Tarot.

The Magician's card stands for a teacher-guide, a person who offers education and enlightenment to all pupils attending the first class in the school of life. The energy embodied in the Magician is that of action, purpose and will. He reveals to the Fool his potentials and possibilities; he lays before him a map of personality in terms of elements, and reminds him of the duality of his nature, mortal and divine. In alchemy, Hermes was said to preside over the whole alchemical work; in the Fool's journey he acts as the initiator and will accompany him, unseen, on his way.

THE MAGICIAN.

In a spread of cards, the Magician indicates an important beginning. It suggests a time for action – creative initiative, skill and potential are in abundance. The equipment needed is available but steps may not yet have been taken towards achievement of the goal. New opportunities for intellectual or creative pursuits are presented, and the possibilities for new ventures seem assured. A great reserve of power and energy is available, it is up to the seeker as to how it is to be used.

THE EMPRESS

It is now time for the Fool to move on and meet the Empress. This card depicts a beautiful, serene woman, seated in the midst of a cornfield and holding a sheaf of corn. She wears full, flowing robes decorated with pomegranates and her long hair is adorned with a twelve-starred crown. Behind her is a forest and a waterfall. The scene is peaceful and calm. The Empress is a symbol of fertility and abundance. She wears full robes as a hint of pregnancy and suggesting potential fulfilled. The pomegranates signify conjugal love and the sheaf of corn is a symbol of fertility. The twelve stars in her crown represent the twelve months of the year, the twelve signs of the zodiac, and the infinite becoming finite in the twelve hours of day and night. She also symbolizes the natural cycles of the year with a time for seed, blossom, fruit and decay. The forest is a symbol of natural richness while the water falling into a pool symbolizes the union of male and female combining to produce new life. The heart-shaped shield by her feet bears the astrological glyph of Venus, ruler of Taurus, the sign associated with nature. Everything about the imagery of this card points to natural growth.

The Empress has much in common with Demeter, the Greek version of Mother Nature. She was the goddess of the earth, ruling all growth, the mistress of motherhood. All young defenceless creatures were believed to be under her benevolent protection. The fruits of the earth, plants, flowers and crops all came under her patronage. As goddess of the fertile soil, Demeter blessed relationships, as well as the fruitfulness of marriage. She was a mother herself, and her daughter, Persephone, was very dear to Demeter's heart. When Persephone was abducted by Hades, King of the Underworld, Demeter was so distraught she forsook her duties as earth goddess and declared she would not resume them until her daughter was returned. During this time the crops failed and no flowers bloomed, so the men and women of the earth went hungry. Finally, with the assistance of diplomatic Hermes, a bargain was struck between Demeter and Hades that Persephone would spend half the year with her mother, during which time the earth rejoiced and bore fruit, and the other half of the year with Hades in the underworld. During the second period Demeter mourned her daughter's absence and the earth was barren.

The Empress represents the Fool's earthly mother. From her he learns about women and their nature. He learns to care and nurture himself and look after his own bodily needs as well as respecting and caring for others. He is loved and cherished by the Empress and is thus able to love and cherish others. He learns about nature, cycles of growth, death and rebirth and he learns about the same cycles operating within men and women and their relationships. Attached as he is to his Empress-mother, he must also learn to leave her and make his own way in the world.

In a reading, the Empress represents happy stable relationships, growth and fertility. It is a symbol for potential fulfilled and a card of love, marriage or motherhood.

THE EMPEROR

If the Empress is the Fool's mother, then who else but the Emperor is his father? Leaving behind the natural feminine softness of the Empress the Fool comes upon the Emperor, who complements her absolutely by portraying quite the opposite characteristics. The Emperor is seated on an impressive stone-carved throne, looking straight ahead. His rich clothing and heavy cloak cover a suit of armour. He wears a jewel-encrusted crown and carries an orb and sceptre. The cloak, concealing armour, suggests that one of the qualities of the Emperor is power beneath which lies considerable strength, available whenever necessary. The jewels symbolize his material wealth and status; the orb he holds represents his rational understanding of the laws necessary for men to abide by. The sceptre is a symbol of his masculine creativity and potency. The image of the Emperor certainly conjures up an impression of authority, power and material wealth.

The Emperor can be associated with Zeus, the supreme father, god of the Greeks. Zeus dispensed good and evil to mankind and gave them rules and morals to abide by. He was capable of much kindness and compassion, although he severely punished those who transgressed his laws. He was thought of by men as just, and could be turned to for a fair decision. Zeus also protected the weak and vulnerable. As we have seen, he fathered Dionysus and took great care to ensure his son's safe birth despite all opposition.

As the Empress is mother, so the Emperor is father, giver of life, sower of the divine seed. The Emperor's task is to teach the Fool to handle the material side of life, how to live and deal in the world of men. He instructs him on matters of authority and administration as well as giving guidelines on moral and ethical behaviour. The wisdom the Emperor imparts is of an earthly nature, but nonetheless essential to the Fool's development. The Emperor is symbolic of a dynamic force, energy chanelled into making ideas solid and workable. He represents the drive for ambition and power, wealth and fame. His mode of expression is direct, forceful and outgoing, unlike his consort the Empress whose feminine energy is receptive and nurturing. The Emperor acts, the Empress is acted upon. The links which form to join the two parents act as a lesson for the Fool that an excess of either quality can be damaging. What is needed is a balance, an equation of the two opposites. The Fool needs to internalize the images and use them in harmony within himself. This theme of balance follows through most of the cards which the Fool encounters and starts with his earthly parents.

In a spread, the Emperor points to material success and stability. He stands for authority. ambition and worldly gain or achievement.

THE HIGH PRIESTESS

The Fool now turns his attention from the earthly plane towards spiritual matters. The time is ripe for him to encounter the mysterious figure of the High Priestess. She stands for his spiritual or celestial mother and is depicted seated between two pillars. Between the pillars hangs a veil decorated with pomegranates through which a glimpse of water can be seen, and a crescent moon lies at her feet. She wears plain blue robes, and sits impassive, hands clasped calmly in her lap, a dramatic contrast to the rich dress and background of the Empress. She bears a scroll which carries the inscription TORA. The two pillars the High Priestess sits between are black and white, symbolizing duality. The feminine nature contains both positive and negative aspects, creative and destructive, benevolent and malevolent, fruitful and barren. The veil of pomegranates, the sacred fruit of Persephone, queen of the underworld, shows the High Priestess's connection with the unconscious world, the realm of the spirit. The glimpse of water beyond the veil symbolizes the hidden riches that lie concealed in the depths of the unconscious mind. The scroll's inscription TORA means natural law, but the letters could be rearranged to read TARO, a clue to the natural wisdom and law contained in the Tarot itself. The ethereal quality of the Priestess contrasts with the earthy richness of the Empress; yet together they combine to form the feminine nature in both its spiritual and earthly sense. The combination of the two is healthy; too much emphasis in either direction leads to imbalance and, as we have seen, the Tarot strives towards balance and wholeness in seeking to achieve integrity of personality.

The High Priestess may be connected with the virgin goddess Persephone, queen of the underworld. The virgin is a symbol of potential yet to be fulfilled. She stands for the treasures of the unconscious mind, brought to consciousness in the same way as Persephone bore Dionysus – Zagreus, god of light. The Priestess can also be connected with Artemis, virgin goddess of the moon, and with Hecate, witch and enchantress, queen of the underworld and of magic. Hecate was goddess of the dark side of the moon and symbolizes the bitter, destructive element in the feminine nature. The bitterness is evoked when the natural potential inherent in the virgin remains unfulfilled.

The High Priestess is connected with occult, secret and esoteric matters, and her emphasis is on unseen talent and potential which needs to be brought to light. All life is started in darkness, whether the darkness of the womb or the soil, and a period of gestation is necessary for the new life to be formed before it is brought to light. An easy example is the foetus developing in the secrecy of the womb until the time is ripe for the fully-formed baby to be born into light. Creative ideas take the same course; the artist or author nurtures the spark of creation long before the imge or idea takes shape in the form of a painting or book. The High Priestess symbolizes the nurturing of spiritual ideas and the knowledge of occult and esoteric matters as well as enchantment and magic, which can be used for good or evil. The duality in her nature is echoed by the black and white pillars. The High Priestess is subtle and unobtrusive, her secrets are not easily read or revealed. The key to understanding her mysteries lies behind the veil in the sea of unconscious. Only by crossing beyond the threshold of consciousness can that which is concealed in darkness be brought to light.

THE HIGH PRIESTESS

The divinatory meanings of this card are: potential as yet unfulfilled; wisdom; secrets to be revealed; occult and esoteric studies; and development of feminine powers of intuition and natural insight.

THE HIEROPHANT

It is time for the Fool to get to know the Hierophant, his heavenly father. The Empress and Emperor form the pair of earthly parents while the High Priestess and the Hierophant join as the Fool's celestial ones. The image of the Hierophant shows him, like the High Priestess, seated between two pillars. However, unlike her, his arms are spread open and he has an audience at his feet. He is clad in priestly robes and blesses the men who kneel before him. Once again, the two pillars are symbolic of duality and the balance that needs to be struck between opposites. The Hierophant has his hand raised with the thumb and first two fingers pointing upwards and the other two fingers folded in on his palm. This indicates the distinction between above and below, gods and men, spirit and matter. The Hierophant stands as a link between the two. Through the priest men obtain knowledge of the spirit and men may communicate with the gods. The keys of heaven are crossed at the foot of the throne, and stand for knowledge of good and evil.

Although the image may depict established religion, the Hierophant's essence seems to be connected in myth with the centaur, Chiron. Chiron was a god who sacrificed his immortality and deserved place on Olympus in exchange for Prometheus's mortality. Prometheus committed the crime against his fellow immortals by stealing divine fire from the gods to give to man. Zeus was enraged by this act of impudence and arranged an agonizing torture as punishment which would last for eternity unless another god was prepared to give up his immortality to rescue Prometheus from his harrowing fate. Chiron obliged for he had a wound he could not heal and wished for mortality so he could die and be released from his pain. He spent his time on earth teaching men spiritual values and instructing them in the art of healing, both spiritual and physical. Chiron guided many heroes and taught many the healing arts.

The Hierophant embodies the other face of the masculine principle. The Emperor stands for man's worldly face while the Hierophant represents his spiritual one. The Hierophant repre-

sents the urge to find spiritual meaning in life; he is the force
behind the forming within each man of religious beliefs or philosophical values. He stands not only for accepted and traditional
theology but also for the need within each man to test out such
teachings or beliefs for himself. The Hierophant is the energy
behind the desire to find a personal spiritual truth. He is thus the
Fool's spiritual guide and mentor, but unlike his partner, the High
Priestess, whose secrets are not readily revealed, the Hierophant is
clearer and more direct in his teachings.

The divinatory meanings of this card are those of assistance
from a wise or helpful person, as well as guidance on spiritual
matters and the need to find spiritual meaning in life.

THE LOVERS

Having completed his childhood under the guidance of his tutor, the Magician, and of his earthly and divine parents, the Fool is now ready to stand at the first trial of youth, namely love.

The image on this card is of a naked man and woman standing in a garden. Behind each is a tree, and above the couple hovers an angel. Between the two in the far distance stands a mountain peak. The scene would appear to reflect Adam and Eve in the Garden of Eden. Behind the man stands the Tree of Life, bearing twelve fruits, one for each sign of the zodiac, while behind the woman stands the Tree of Knowledge, from which hangs five fruits representing the five senses. The couple face each other, yet the man looks towards the woman while she looks towards the angel, which implies that the masculine principle of intellect cannot reach the spirit directly but only through the feminine principle of emotion. The angel holds out his arms as if to draw the pair together, for only together can they reach the mountain which stands between them. The mountain has to be climbed to reach its peak, and each partner has an equal distance to travel to obtain harmony with the other, symbolized by the mountain. There are important choices to be made at ground level before the journey can commence. It seems as if the couple, wishing to journey towards a life of harmony together, have to make choices and be prepared to leave the safety of the garden in which they innocently stand.

The image of Adam and Eve as the Lovers' trump is Waite's own design and varies considerably from the image the older packs carry and which depicts an important myth. This image is of a young man apparently trying to choose between two or even three women while Cupid hovers above, pointing his bow and arrow at the young man's heart. The Greek myth upon which this Trump is thought to have been based, is the Judgement of Paris. Paris was a mortal, but one day while tending his sheep, he unwittingly became involved in a dispute among the gods. A beauty contest was being held between the three great goddesses, Athena, Hera and Aphrodite. Each felt she deserved the title 'the fairest', and they squabbled so violently among themselves that Zeus finally demanded that Paris should be the judge. Each of the goddesses turned to him, offering glittering promises to tempt him and sway his judgement. Hera offered to make him lord of all Asia; Athena promised that he would be successful in every battle he fought; but Aphrodite, goddess of love and beauty, merely unclasped her magic girdle which made her irresistible. As if that were not enough, Paris's heart was pierced by Eros's (Cupid's) golden arrows and he was smitten with love and desire. He handed Aphrodite the prize without question, and in return the goddess promised to him the hand of the most beautiful woman on earth. This woman turned out to be none other than Helen of Troy, who unfortunately was already married. The terrible Trojan war broke out when Paris tried to claim his prize.

THE LOVERS.

This myth illustrates the dangers and pitfalls which attend all choices, particularly those made in the name of love. The Fool must learn that love is not a simple matter decided by physical attraction, and that the considerations made in affairs of the heart are neither easy nor straightforward. The Fool must learn also that any choice in love will inevitably bring about repercussions and complications, just like the ripples caused from a single pebble dropped into a pool.

In a layout, the Lovers indicates a relationship or love affair but with some sort of trial or choice involved. Marriage may follow such a choice, or it may be what the old books described as 'the choice between sacred and profane love'.

THE CHARIOT

The Fool, having struggled with love's complexities, is now ready to encounter war, the next trial of youth. The image of the Chariot stands in stark contrast to the Lovers, where the figures are naked and unprotected, suggesting the only way to explore the complex realms of love. However, the Chariot shows a figure clad in shining armour, upright in his vehicle of battle. The Chariot is drawn by two sphinxes, one black, the other white, with four pillars supporting a canopy made up of blue star-spangled cloth. The sphinxes are a symbol of an enigma or riddle which the charioteer must solve, each sphinx reflecting an opposite nature indicated by their different colours. The four pillars stand for the four elements; the starry canopy depicts the heavens, while the body of the Chariot represents the earth, thereby symbolizing the ancient magical dictum 'as above, so below'. As the Chariot is a vehicle of battle it seems appropriate to connect this card with Ares, the Greek god of war.

Ares was a passionate, fiery-tempered god who always seemed to be involved in one skirmish or another. His method of fighting was to use brute strength, and it might indeed have been his masculine strength and pride which attracted Aphrodite, goddess of love. The Warrior and the Lover are said to walk hand in hand, and in Greek myth Ares and Aphrodite were lovers. Their union bore a child named Harmonia, or Harmony, symbolizing the positive result of reuniting and reconciling opposites.

This card is about the conflict which opposites create. The card depicts the charioteer keeping the opposing sphinxes under control. Each is a different colour, so each will want to pull in a different direction. It is the charioteer's job to stop them pulling too far out of control, or from turning on one another. These opposite forces are often thought to be the carnal and spiritual forces within man which need to be balanced. They can also represent the wish to go forward and the simultaneous wish to stay secure in the tried and tested. The Fool, as the charioteer, must learn how to steer a middle course through the battleground of his opposing feelings, thoughts and desires. Although uncomfortable, the confusion brought about by the opposition can be creative, for conflict is necessary to promote change and growth. No change results in stagnation.

In a reading, the Chariot represents the quality of energy needed to fight for a desired goal. It shows a struggle or conflict of interests, and can mean a fight for self-assertion is necessary. However, if well placed in the spread, a successful outcome is assured as is triumph over difficulties and obstacles.

The Minor Arcana

The Fool has completed the first leg of his journey through the Major Trumps, so it seems an appropriate time to take a look at the Minor Arcana. The pack was used to illustrate the text designed by A.E. Waite and drawn by Pamela Coleman-Smith under Waite's direction around 1900. This deck owes a lot of its symbolism to the teachings of the Order of the Golden Dawn. This was a secret society of magicians and mystics to which Waite and Coleman-Smith both belonged. The Minor Arcana of the Waite deck differs from the other, older decks because of its descriptive imagery. The Order of the Golden Dawn attributed the four suits of the Minor Arcana to the elements and numbers of the cabalistic Tree of Life. The four suits were connected with the Hebrew letters of the alphabet Y–H–V–H which denoted the name of God. The letters were in turn connected with each of the four elements thus: Y–Fire–Wands stands for the initial spark of creative energy which commences any project or living thing; the first H–Water–Cups adds emotion and feeling to this process, but until V–Air–Swords, standing for intellect and power of thought is added, the energy and emotions remain unorganized. The final H–Earth–Pentacles stands for the operation of making the end-product real in physical terms by giving it structure and form.

If we take each element and suit as representative of a psychological function, as conceived of by C.J. Jung, we can elaborate on the basic energies contained in each card. Let us look at each suit and card in turn.

WANDS–FIRE–INTUITION

Fire is the energy which in psychological terms is called intuition. It is the spark of divine creativity, the feeling of inspiration and inner certainty which forms an important beginning for the whole creative process. Fire is the faith in one's ability to have 'brain-waves', and to be able to make something out of a passing thought or day-dream. Intuition is connected with imagination and the world of creative fantasy. Without the other elements to balance and stabilize this energy, however, the creativity may fizzle out through lack of form.

CUPS–WATER–FEELING

Water symbolizes the feelings and emotions which give depth to the creative urge represented by Fire. Fire is active, male, life-giving energy while Water is passive, feminine and nurturing. Water represents the feelings and emotions which are constantly shifting expression. In the suit of cups, the Water element seems to refer mainly to love and relationships, happy or otherwise. The suit deals with inner experiences and emotions. In the same way that uncontained Fire may simply fizzle out, uncontained Water may overwhelm and drown that which is most valuable within.

SWORDS–AIR–THINKING

Air is represented by the Swords, the suit connected with strife and difficulty. Air and intellect seek out the truth and logic in life. The cutting edge of the intellect depicted by the Swords can slice through deception and illusion which may be painful, but things seen and understood can be things accepted. Thinking is an essential function in being able to sort out muddled ideas and emotions, and the more confused we become the more we need the sharp edge of the Sword to cut through to the truth.

PENTACLES–EARTH–SENSATION

Earth is a symbol for our bodies, our physical being, our physical needs. The earth itself provides the firm base from which we can grow. From the intuitive conception of an idea, through its emotional importance, tested by the intellect, the earth finally provides a basis for the idea to develop into reality. The element Earth is the essential base on which foundations for creative, emotional or intellectual ideas can be established. These can be made solid and brought to concrete form through the earth-plane or sensation function. The symbol of the five-pointed star, engraved on each pentacle, is a magical glyph symbolizing the earthy magic found in our bodies, in nature and in the world.

This brief glance at the suits and their elements should make it clear that each is essential but none can be of any real value without the balancing influence of all the others. I have chosen to take each number in each suit and study them as a group, it is interesting and helpful to get the feel of each number and observe how each expresses itself differently through the four elements. We will start with the Aces and work up to the Tens and then look at the court cards.

The Aces

The Ace or Number One is the beginning of all things. One is the number of creative power and potential. It is the primary number from which all the others grow. All the Aces show a tremendous upsurge of energy; they indicate new beginnings of a vital, positive and vigorous nature.

Ace of Wands

The image on this card shows a strong hand, emerging from a cloud, offering a budding Wand. The distance reveals a castle on a hill, a promise of what the future might bring. Wands correspond to fire, the element of creativity, energy and initiative, and the Ace suggests positive new beginnings and ideas along such lines. The Aces stand for energy in its purest form, so the Ace of Wands represents pure creativity. This card can symbolize a new business venture, a new undertaking, new foundations and creative power with plenty of potential and ambition to progress and succeed.

Ace of Cups

A hand appears from the clouds, this time bearing a beautiful Cup. The image seems to have been inspired by the Grail legends, as a dove symbolizing spiritual values descends holding a communion wafer in its beak. Five streams of water, which stand for the five senses, spring from the cup and fall into a lily pond. The water lily is a symbol of emotional growth. The Cups are con-

ACE of CUPS.

nected with water, the element governing feelings and emotions, so the Ace of Cups means the purest aspect of emotional energy. It can indicate the beginning of a new relationship, the renewal of strong emotions, love, marriage, motherhood, and great joy or reward gained from a loving union.

Ace of Swords

This card depicts the two-edged sword which cuts both ways. It is circled by a crown, a symbol of attainment, from which hangs an olive branch, symbol of peace, and a palm leaf standing for victory. The Swords correspond to the element Air, and to the intellect. They also point to strife and difficulty. The Ace of Swords is a card of strength in adversity, and often indicates that out of evil something good will come. A situation that looks bleak can surprisingly turn out to be extremely promising. A sense of inevitable change comes with this card, 'the old order changeth'. It is a card of great power, force and strength.

Ace of Pentacles

This time the hand from the clouds offers a golden pentacle. A well-cared-for garden beneath indicates the positive reward for

hard work. The Pentacles correspond with earth, the element of the body, matter and material gain. It can also stand for worldly status and achievement, as well as for financial security or wealth. The Ace signifies good beginnings for financial propositions, business ventures or enterprises. It can mean the successful founding of a business which will bring financial rewards, prosperity and security firmly based. It might also indicate a lump sum of money or gifts, perhaps of gold.

The Twos

The number Two reveals opposites: positive and negative, male and female, spirit and matter, and so on. The pure energy of the Aces is split into opposing forces of conflict or balance. The duality of the twos manifests in the cards that follow either as a balance of forces or a creativity not yet fulfilled.

Two of Wands

As we have seen in the Ace, the Wands signify enterprise, energy and growth. The man depicted in the card stands on castle walls,

two wands placed firmly in the ground, symbolizing what he had already achieved. He holds a tiny globe in one hand which stands for the future possibilities. He seems to be trying to decide his next move. The design on his castle battlements consists of white lilies, representing pure thought, and red roses, a symbol of desire. The combination indicates well-balanced nature, but the essence of the card remains potential as yet unfulfilled. The card denotes high ideals and aims, a desire for travel and a new outlook from present environment. There is change in the air and a feeling of restlessness. The card promises success through strength and vision; initiative can overcome obstacles.

Two of Cups

This card is a good example of the balance of opposites: a man and woman exchanging cups. The Cups are symbols of love and emotion, the pure energy of which overflowed in the Ace. Now

the energy is divided; two people are involved and both their interests need to be considered. The serpents of good and evil entwine around the staff as emblems of love's positive and negative attributes while the lion, usually associated with carnal desire, has the wings of the spirit, indicating a happy balance between spiritual and physical love. This card denotes the beginning of a romance or well-balanced friendship. Ideas are generated between the two partners with harmony and co-operation. The card can indicate an engagement, or commitment to romance or friendship. It can mean reconciliation of opposites or the resolution of quarrels and disputes.

Two of Swords

A blindfolded woman is seated at the water's edge, holding two swords in perfect balance. The blindfold indicates that she cannot see her way through her present situation, so she steadfastly ignores the sea of her emotions and the jagged rocks of hard facts behind her. The swords she raises are well balanced for the moment, but she is in a precarious situation. This is the card of stalemate: the balanced forces have immobilized each other. The conflict has reached an impasse. The person is so frightened, or unsure of which way to turn or move, that he does nothing at all

except try to ignore it. It is as though the person feels by not confronting the issues at hand they might go away. However, with courage, a change can be made, and often good comes out of what appears to be a bad situation.

Two of Pentacles

A young man is balancing two pentacles quite happily although behind him the sea is rough. Nevertheless, he appears light-hearted as he casually juggles the pentacles. This card stands for

the necessity to keep several propositions going at once. The flow of movement, however, indicates that skilful manipulation achieves success. There is change, particularly with regard to financial matters, but also harmony within the change if the person can be flexible enough to keep everything moving.

The Threes

Three is the number of growth and expansion. Number One

contains the idea, Number Two is the pair who can carry out the idea and Number Three bears the fruit of the partnership. The Three is the number of initial completion, the first stage achieved.

Three of Wands

The same man depicted in the Two reappears. He looks out over much wider horizons and has now staked three wands in the ground. He has made his decision and now he can proceed further still. Efforts are rewarded in this card and an initial completion of some work or goal is achieved. It is like a person who works single-mindedly at a job until it is finished and who then has to take stock, for the next phase follows fast. It is a card of satisfaction and challenge at the same time, for although one thing is achieved, there is much more yet to do.

Three of Cups

Three maidens dance and hold high their cups in joyful celebration. Fruit and flowers in abundance lie at their feet. The image

clearly depicts a celebration or joyful occasion. It can signify a marriage or birth, emotional growth, and a feeling of happiness and achievement. It can also indicate the conclusion of a happy matter or a healing of wounds. As with all the Threes, however, there is a sense that it's important to enjoy the moment of rejoicing for there is still hard work ahead. This is only the beginning.

Three of Swords

Rain and clouds form the background for a heart pierced by three swords, which makes a gloomy picture. This card indicates stormy weather for the emotions. There may be quarrels or separations as a result; maybe tears over a faithless lover. There is a sense of clearing the ground for something new, however, amid the sorrow, for the 'darkest hour is before the dawn'. This card signifies a flash of understanding or insight into a situation as it really is, which helps to put the sorrow in perspective. This card can also mean that the difficulties experienced in relationships can be overcome if faced honestly and worked with.

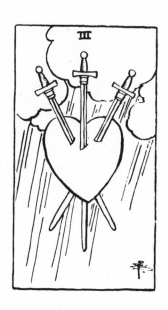

Three of Pentacles

This card shows a craftsman discussing plans with two people. They appear to be talking over ideas for the next phase of work.

Once again, the initial completion of work is achieved. A structure is finished with; now the finer details are to be added. The basic form or structure is sound and complete, so finishing touches can now be added. The card may denote material gain or success through effort. Approval and recognition may be given by others and a sense of achievement can be deservedly experienced.

The Fours

The number Four makes up a square, with each side equal. It is the number of reality, logic and reason. The essence of man's three-fold nature – mind, body and spirit – is brought to the material plane, forming a square.

The Four of Wands

Garlands of flowers form a triumphal arch for the approaching couple, who hold their bouquets high. Behind them is a bridge over a moat, leading to a castle symbolising success. Here we have

the solidity of the Four mingled with the energy and growth characteristic of the Wands; so the result is a happy and productive card.

The satisfaction of the 'harvest home' is indicated by the card: celebration and reward after labour, a pause in activities and a tranquil time of rest. There may be holidays due, or a time of relaxation.

Four of Cups

A young man sits cross-legged, arms folded discontentedly, gazing at three cups before him. He ignores or refuses a fourth cup offered by a hand in a cloud. He seems caught between the world of thought and action, for the volatile nature of the feelings is not happy in the solidity of the number four.

The card is one of 'divine discontent'. The young man has a lot going for him, as shown by the three cups before him, and yet more is offered in a magical way, but he is too bored, confused or unhappy to see the good around him, or benefit by taking the opportunities offered. There is too much discontent in him, and

he turns his emotions inwards. He needs to look at his life in a fresh way and reassess his position.

Four of Swords

The image on this card is of an effigy of a knight in repose over his tomb, his hands clasped in prayer. Three swords hang over him; the fourth is fastened to his tomb.

Although the image looks threatening, the meaning of this card is a time of rest or retreat after a struggle: a quiet period for thinking things through, a slackening of tension and a relaxation of anxiety. A time of convalescence or recuperation.

Four of Pentacles

The man depicted on this card holds on tightly to the gold he has earned. This card couples the strength of purpose of the number four with the monetary aspect of the pentacle.

It is a card which means 'nothing ventured nothing gained' The man holds on to his gold and risks nothing; nor does he gain.

Five of Cups

A figure in a black cloak sorrows over three spilt cups of wine. Behind him remain two upright cups but he does not notice them.

This can apply to whatever he holds dear, and can also mean miserliness with regard to love and emotion as well as money. A risk might need to be taken in order to get things moving again.

The Fives

The Five is the number of uncertainty. It carries no constant vibration and may change or shift, though it seems that the five in Tarot signifies more adversity than it does in numerology.

Five of Wands

Five young men are depicted brandishing huge wands in combat, and a conflict of interest is aptly pictured. A struggle in life and love is suggested, for this card indicates petty obstacles and annoyances, short-term difficulties in communication which, once overcome, can change things for the better. In the short term it seems as if nothing works out quite right in work and play.

He can only concentrate on what has been spilled. There may be regret over past actions, something is lost but something still remains. The person needs to look at what can be salvaged, for the two upright cups are full. There are new alternatives to be explored within the loss.

Five of Swords

A man stands victorious in battle while two defeated warriors slink away. The victor seems invincible and the other men have no choice but to surrender their swords to him. The message this card

gives is to swallow false pride and accept limitations before moving upwards and onwards. The person needs to give up fighting and try something which he can win. He is banging his head against a brick wall in continuing to fight, and is taking on something too big. The card advises acknowledging limitation and proceeding in a new direction.

Five of Pentacles

Two beggars pass under a lighted church window. They walk in the snow, one lame, the other appears destitute. They do not seem to notice the light above for their heads are bowed down in sorrow. Here is the reverse of the usual good fortune which so often appears in the Pentacles. There may be strain or anxiety over money, a warning that financial hard times are ahead temporarily. This message may be deeper than just lack of money, for the beggars in this card may also have lost spiritual direction symbolized by their inability to get comfort and shelter within the church. The card urges the seeker to pay attention to detail, financial, emotional or spiritual, for there is a warning that without due care something important or valuable may otherwise be lost.

EXERCISES

The Major Arcana

Now that you have completed the first part, you have an opportunity to get to know your cards more deeply. This first exercise is all about getting to know the Fool. Extract the Fool card from your pack and study it carefully. Look closely at his clothing, at what he is doing, the feel of card, and all other details that strike you. Make a note of your first reactions. Now, try to identify with the Fool; put yourself in his place: you are at the beginning of a journey into the new and exciting world of Tarot. The Fool is about to take a leap off the edge of a precipice into the unknown, strange territory that lies below him. Imagine the feelings and thoughts that might be flashing through his mind as he stands poised on the edge. Would his feelings be similar to those going through YOUR mind as YOU start on your journey into the Tarot? You may be nervous, as is the Fool, but like him you stand to gain greater benefit as a result of daring to take on this challenge. Go on, JUMP!

Now think about the following questions and either write them out or tape them to keep some record of your initial reactions:

a) How would you describe yourself as you embark on your journey?
b) What do you hope to gain?
c) What do you have in common with the Fool?

Now is the time for you to tackle a 'guided fantasy' exercise. The first and most important thing to do is leave yourself free time in which you will be quite undisturbed. Take the telephone off the hook and make yourself comfortable. Sit or lie down, whichever position you feel most relaxed in, and take several deep breaths. Relax every muscle in your body as fully as you can. Close your eyes and clear your mind, try to empty it of all the day's events and your week's worries. When you feel peaceful and at ease, take the Magician card and look at it closely. Keep looking at the picture until you can see it with your eyes closed. Now try to imagine the card surround as a window frame. Imagine yourself climbing into the window frame to stand alongside the Magician. Imagine him as a real live figure. See the fabric of his robes; see the glinting of the gold and metal objects on his table; smell the perfume from the roses and lilies in his garden. Now imagine that you are holding a conversation with him. Ask him questions, listen carefully to his answers. Talk for as long as you like, but when you feel ready to bid him farewell make sure that you 'close the fantasy down' properly by climbing back out of the window and imagine the image as a card again. This is an important part of the exercise. When you are ready to open your eyes write down or record your talk with him. Note your feelings and thoughts about the meeting with care. The more of a personal record you can build up the better rapport you can expect with you cards. It may seem awkward at first, and you may even feel foolish, but if you persevere, this imaginary exercise will conjure up many different thoughts and associations for you personally with each card. It is the best way to get in tune with your pack and with the cards' meanings.

Now repeat this exercise with all the other Major Arcana cards we've looked at so far, but obviously in your own time. The important thing to remember is that you really need to set aside enough time to be alone and relax fully in order to get maximum benefit. As with any study, it takes time and effort but it is extremely worthwhile when done properly.

The Minor Arcana

Go through all the numbers we have looked at so far, and try to associate the essence or feeling of the card with something from your personal experience. For instance, does a particular card remind you of the first time you fell in love, lost your job, moved house? Note whatever comes to mind when you study each card. If you can jot down your immediate reactions, so much the better. The hard work you put in now will reward you richly when you start doing readings.

PART TWO

JUSTICE
TEMPERANCE
STRENGTH
THE HERMIT
THE WHEEL OF FORTUNE
THE HANGED MAN

SIXES
SEVENS
EIGHTS
NINES
TENS

Now let us continue with the next stage of the Fool's journey. He has received the benefits of his education with his teacher and parents; he has learned lessons in love and war and is now ready to face what are known as the four moral lessons, namely Justice, Temperance, Strength and Prudence (the Hermit).

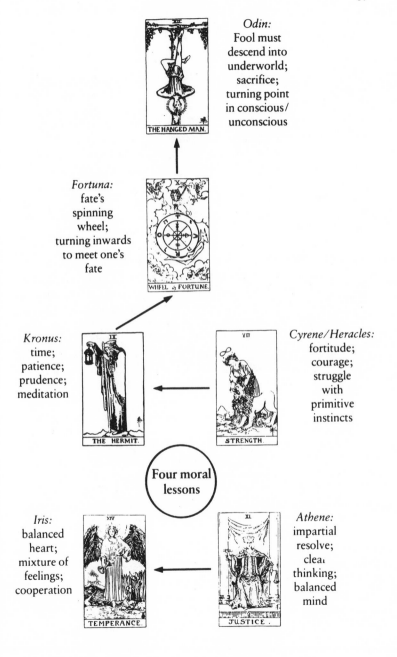

Odin:
Fool must descend into underworld; sacrifice; turning point in conscious/unconscious

THE HANGED MAN.

Fortuna: fate's spinning wheel; turning inwards to meet one's fate

WHEEL of FORTUNE.

Kronus: time; patience; prudence; meditation

THE HERMIT.

Cyrene/Heracles: fortitude; courage; struggle with primitive instincts

STRENGTH.

Four moral lessons

Iris: balanced heart; mixture of feelings; cooperation

TEMPERANCE.

Athene: impartial resolve; clear thinking; balanced mind

JUSTICE.

JUSTICE

The Fool now attends the school of Justice. The figure on this card is pictured between two pillars wearing a red robe and a green cloak. A purple veil hangs between the pillars. She is an imposing figure, staring straight ahead, a golden crown upon her head, her right hand holding a sword and her left, a pair of scales. The two pillars, which are reminiscent of those on the High Priestess and the Hierophant cards, depict the eternal opposites, and the purple veil between them is the colour of wisdom. Red is the colour of war, while green is the colour of love, and her dress combines to symbolize the harmony inherent in a balance of opposites. The sword is masculine and the scales, feminine, again denoting balance between male and female. The zodiac sign of Libra, associated with balance, uses scales as its symbol.

The figure on the Justice card may be connected with Athene, the wise goddess of Greece. She used the power of the intellect to its fullest capacity; and although a warrior goddess, she fought battles using the application of intellect and strategy rather than brute force. This card, in contrast to the Chariot, shows that battle can be won using brain not brawn. Athene was venerated as goddess of prudent intelligence. She was protector of heroes, and guided many on perilous expeditions. One story tells of a contest between herself and the god of the ocean, Poseidon, in which each had to produce a precious gift to man. The gods on Olympus would judge which gift could be most useful to the human race. Poseidon struck open the ground with his powerful trident, and out sprang the first horse that the gods and men had ever seen. The gods were most impressed and indeed doubted that Athene could produce anything to match it; however Athene presented them with an olive tree, the first of its kind, and quietly informed the assembly of its many virtues. The fruit and its oil were useful to nourish man's body but, more importantly, the leaf was an emblem of peace, while the horse was a symbol of war. Athene duly won the contest and the city of Athens was named after her.

Justice teaches the Fool to discriminate, to make dispassionate evaluations and the impersonal decisions that the intellect is concentrated upon at this stage of his journey; he must learn to solve his problems impartially, to weigh up, to balance and then to make rational judgements. Justice is a fundamentally human conception centring on fairness and reason. Nature, however, is not fair, nor is it reasonable, according to man's interpretation of the word. Even so, man at his best strives to be fair and to use justice in an attempt to establish equilibrium as a guiding principle of his world and on his society. Although his ideal might seem hopelessly naïve, because nature can never be tamed by man, justice is nevertheless one of the most noble conceptions of the human spirit.

In a reading, Justice stands for the need to weigh things up, to find fair and rational solutions, for reason and thought to override emotion, although at times Justice might need to be tempered with mercy, as we will see in the next card. In short, it stands for the need for a balanced mind.

TEMPERANCE

The Fool has learned the value of a balanced mind which he now needs to complement with a balanced heart. He meets the angel of Temperance, dressed in pure white robes with huge rainbow-coloured wings. The angel is pouring water from a golden cup into a silver one, and stands with one foot on land, the other in the water. A road leads away from the pool towards twin mountain peaks, between which the sun is rising. Beside the pool grow beautiful irises. The angel's wings hint at his supernatural quality, and he pours the waters of emotions from the golden cup, symbolizing consciousness, into the silver one, standing for the unconscious, thus showing the need for a constant flow between the two; water which does not flow stagnates, as do feelings. The placement of the angel's feet echoes this, as land and water are associated with the conscious and the unconscious, respectively. The road leading to the mountains represents a route for the Fool to follow, and the rising sun offers new hope in the task of resolving opposites, represented by the twin peaks. The irises growing by the pool are the flower of the goddess of the rainbow. The rainbow is a popular symbol of promise and hope, expressed in folklore as a 'pot of gold at the end of the rainbow' or in children's songs as a land beyond the rainbow where dreams come true.

The Temperance angel is connected with Iris, the messenger goddess of the rainbow, who served both Zeus and Hera. The rainbow bridges heaven and earth so Iris was equally at ease on earth, in the sky or even in the ocean's depth, where she would cheerfully descend to carry messages. She was a kind and compassionate goddess whose willingness to help everyone made her beloved of gods and men alike. It was said that even the underworld opened up at her feet when she was sent by Zeus to refill her golden cup with the waters of the river Styx.

The Fool learns through this card how to mix, in their due proportions, the opposites of success and failure, growth and decay, joy and sorrow; the waters poured by the angel represent these different feelings and emotions. The care with which they are poured shows the benefit of moderation. Justice may need to be tempered with mercy, and Temperance offers the quality of compassion and forgiveness; taking into account the feelings in situations rather than just the factual circumstances, as Justice does. The feelings strive towards a sense of calm and serenity, the equivalent of what the mind knows as Justice.

In a reading, Temperance stands for cooperation, successful blending of opposites and signifies compromise in marriage and partnerships. It is the card denoting balanced emotions.

STRENGTH

The Fool has gained experience in thought and feeling; now he needs to develop the capacity to control, discipline and weigh up these elements within himself. The card of Strength depicts a beautiful maiden in flowing white robes, her hair adorned with a wreath of flowers while garlands entwine her waist. She stands in a lush green meadow, the very picture of femininity, yet incongruously she is bending over a lion, firmly yet kindly closing his jaw. Once again, this imagery shows the blend and union of opposites in the maiden who represents the Moon and femininity, with the lion who symbolizes the Sun and masculinity. The maiden is not trying to kill the lion, only tame him, and the lion, symbol of strength and power, is submitting to her. There is no evidence of force, yet the lion meekly obeys the maiden's firm command.

Greek myth tells of Apollo, the Sun god, encountering Cyrene, handmaiden to the Moon goddess Artemis, struggling with a fierce lion. Cyrene won her fight, and Apollo was so charmed with her courage and fortitude, as well as her feminine beauty, that he spirited her off to a paradise land where she enjoyed harmony and peace ever afterward. Some Tarot decks show Herakles struggling with the Nemean lion which he tried in vain to kill with arrows. He finally resorted to a hand-to-hand fight and succeeded in strangling the beast. He kept its skin, however, and wore it as a cloak of protection which rendered him invulnerable. A large number of fairy tales and myths tell of a hero's journey or quest which involves him meeting a wild animal who helps him, but the hero must first tame the animal before it can become a travelling companion.

These myths are useful when looking at the psychological lesson this card offers. The lion stands for instinctive desires and wishes, which, although they should not be denied or repressed, sometimes need to be controlled. A child does not have this sense of self control from birth; it is something which is acquired during the development of personality. A child needs to learn that it is not always appropriate to do as he pleases when he pleases, and must therefore acquire some self-discipline. This is not the same as denying the impulse altogether. Herakles struggles with the lion and kills it, but wears its skin as protection. The beast within must be acknowledged and integrated for it to be of use. This card represents the strength and endurance necessary to achieve self-control. It suggests that obstacles can be overcome through will-power resulting in a sense of mastery. Leo is the zodiac sign which represents individuality and self mastery, and uses the lion as its emblem.

In a reading, the card shows courage, strength and deter-minaiton. It offers the possibility of achieving self-awareness, strength and determination. It stands for potential integration and individuality.

THE HERMIT

After the colour and vibrance of the previous cards, the Fool comes upon the grey stillness of the Hermit. Although this card displays the dullest colours of any of the Major Trumps, it does not mean it is symbolic of dullness or stagnation. It depicts an old man, head bowed down, shrouded in a grey hooded cloak. Only his hands and the top of his face are exposed. He has a long white beard and holds a staff in his left hand, a mysterious figure standing alone against a grey horizon. Even the earth's natural richness seems to have deserted this sombre figure; all that can be seen of a landscape is a snow-clad mountain ridge. The only thing that offers him light and warmth is his lantern which he holds in his right hand and which emanates a warm, golden glow. His sturdy staff offers and symbolizes support.

This card can be connected with Cronus, who, legend tells us, ruled the Golden Age of Man, and, to avoid giving up his reign of this special time, swallowed all his children at birth for fear they might overthrow him. However, his wife, Rhea, finally exasperated at producing children for her husband to dispose of in this unfriendly manner, tricked Cronus into swallowing a stone wrapped in swaddling clothes. The real baby boy, Zeus, grew to manhood in secrecy but finally claimed his right to rule, banishing Cronus to the Isles of the Blessed, where he ruled peacefully as the god of time and old age. The story ends by adding that if Cronus waits patiently enough the Golden Age will come back.

The image of the Hermit, with its starkness and lack of detailed imagery, pulls us up short. However, this card clearly indicates that the time is ripe for withdrawal from the busy outside world in order to enter the quiet inner one. This means clearing our minds of the external hurly-burly to allow time and space for our minds to empty and our thoughts to clear. The Hermit teaches the lesson of time and the inevitability of old age. Time and change must be accepted as part of the natural cycle by which man lives, for they involve constant flow from birth to blossom to fruit, to return to the seed to ground.

Another sobering lesson the Hermit teaches is that of solitude, another of man's great fears. The truth is, ultimately, that we are all always alone, but to face this fact is often frightening and uncomfortable. At the same time, however, by facing the truth we are half-way to accepting it, and once it is accepted it stops being so frightening. Cronus did not wish to grow old and refused to accept his limitations, but eventually, during his enforced solitary exile, he found inner peace and became content to let time take its course. Acceptance, patience and inner understanding are the messages brought by the Hermit.

In a reading, he represents a time for soul-searching and meditation, the need for patience and a time to work things out quietly. A degree of solitude is often needed.

THE WHEEL OF FORTUNE

The Fool now reaches the turning point in his journey. He is at the point where he realizes that there is more to life, and to himself, than the external world. He glimpsed this during his time with the Hermit, and now, as the Wheel of Fortune turns, he realizes there is a whole new world beneath the surface which he has not yet visited.

The image on the card shows a wheel supported by a strange creature, half man and half jackal. He is connected with Anubis, the Egyptian god who, like the Greek Hermes, was a Conductor of Souls. Anubis would take the dead by the hand and lead them into the presence of judges who would weigh the soul before passing sentence. The snake represents Set, Egyptian god of evil, who was supposed to have brought death to the world. Astride the wheel is seated a sphinx, symbolizing resurrection, and life emerging triumphant over death. The creatures in the four corners of the card are the four fixed signs of the zodiac: Aquarius, Taurus, Leo and Scorpio, which also stand for the four elements: earth, air, fire and water. The symbols on the inner circle are alchemical and stand for mercury, sulphur, water and salt, the essential ingredients required for the great alchemical works. The letters TORA, or if read in reverse, TARO, mark the four compass points of the circle.

In many other packs, the Wheel of Fortune has a different image, slightly easier to comprehend. It depicts a blindfolded woman turning a wheel, at the compass point of which are figures respectively rising, crowning, falling and having fallen off the wheel. This symbolizes the goddess Fortuna who blindly turns the wheel of fate according to which man's fortunes rise and fall. The figures on the wheel symbolize rising towards success, achieving it, losing it and being without success at all, which is again reflected in the cycle of life: birth, blossom, fruition, death.

The Wheel of Fortune is a symbol of stability and change. The true self of a man, which is hidden from his conscious mind, very often remains at the still hub of the wheel, like the blind goddess. The hub remains stable though the external or conscious situations change, as reflected by the moving outer rim. Fate is the moving circumference of the Wheel, while the true self is the centre. The hub enables the rim to turn and is thus responsible for all that comes its way. Each man is responsible for his own destiny, and although circumstances are determined, as are the four points of the great wheel, it is each man who turns his own wheel to whichever point his true self dictates. So, when joy or sorrow come into your life it is not that misfortune or happiness have *befallen* you, but rather that you have turned to face it. Fate does not seek you out, you turn to meet your fate. Often, the fear of taking such a responsibility upon our own shoulders causes us to blame fate for the course our lives take. In reality, we are presented with choices and situations, and what we do with them is on our own account. This is the difficult lesson the Fool learns at the Wheel of Fortune and he must now take responsibility for his own life and fate.

When the Wheel appears in a spread, it signifies a new chapter is starting, a decision of importance is to be made, a new run of luck is commencing. The more you are aware of your own power over your destiny, the clearer things will appear.

THE HANGED MAN

At this point, the Fool starts his descent into the underworld to explore the realms of his subconscious. He confronts a strange figure suspended by one leg, the other tucked behind to form an inverted triangle. His face looks serene even though his position appears uncomfortable and a halo shines brightly around his head. The Hanged Man thus appears to be suspended voluntarily from the tree and the inverted triangle formed by his legs suggests the descent of high nature into the lower, or conscious into unconscious. The halo symbolizes light shining in the darkness of the underworld.

The essential meaning of this card is one of sacrifice: the voluntary giving up of something in order to get something of greater value. In Teutonic myth, the god Odin volunteered his own sacrifice and rejuvenation. 'For nine nights,' he says in an old poem, 'wounded by my own spear, consecrated to Odin, myself consecrated to myself, I remained hanging from the tree, shaken by the wind, from the mighty tree whose roots men know not.' The tree mentioned was the ash Yggdrasil, the world tree, and by wounding himself and hanging from its branches, Odin performed a magical rite for the purpose of rebirth and rejuvenation. As he hung for those nine lonely days and nights, he waited in vain for someone to bring him food or drink. However, as he hung he looked about carefully at what lay beneath him and noticed some runes – characters carved on stone which have magical meaning and powers. He managed with some considerable effort to pick one up and was immediately released from the tree by their magic. He was filled anew with youth and vigour; and so his resurrection and rejuvenation was accomplished.

The Fool has reached the point in his journey at which knowledge of what lies within becomes as important, if not more so, than what exists outside. This card represents the turning point in psychological development where the individual must come to grips with unconscious forces within him. He needs to sacrifice control of his conscious ego by surrendering to the unknown territory of his inner world. It seems this can only be done by conscious choice; it cannot be inflicted by others or by the outside world, although circumstances may contribute to one wanting to look within. As Jung† says, it is as if the conscious mind volunteers to die in order to bear a new and fruitful life in the unconscious, despite the fears of the unknown and the fear that inevitably arises when a journey to the underworld of Hades is contemplated. The Fool started his journey with a sense of trust and willingness to take a risk no matter what, and now, once again, he has to take a risk and dare to make that inner journey.

In a reading, the Hanged Man indicates a time of greater understanding. It also indicates that a sacrifice will have to be made, although it is worth remembering that the sacrifice will be made in order to gain something of greater value.

THE HANGED MAN.

---

†Jung, C. G. Psychology and Alchemy. Routledge and Kegan Paul, London, 1953.

We have now completed two-thirds of the Major cards and are ready to start work on the next group of Minor cards. The numbers we will be looking at now are Six, Seven, Eight, Nine and Ten.

The Sixes

The Six is the number of equilibrium, harmony and balance. The six-pointed star is formed out of two triangles, one pointing up towards the spirit or heavens, and the other pointing down towards the body or earth, which symbolizes balance between them.

Six of Wands

A man on horseback is crowned with a laurel wreath of success and triumph. Another wreath is attached to his wand and people

mill around him in admiration, applauding his success. This card is one of achievement, fulfilment of hopes and wishes in one's career, and great satisfaction. Acclaim is received from others, and due recognition is awarded for success. It can mean promotion after good work, or reward for effort expended in a good cause.

Six of Cups

A boy is offering a little girl a cup filled with flowers. Nearby stand five more flower-filled cups, and, behind the pair, a thatched cottage and quaint old village green conveys thoughts of home and childhood memories. The Six of Cups can bring a meeting with an old friend or childhood acquaintance; an old lover may reappear or a love affair with roots in the past may be revived. This card can also mean that something with roots in the past may be reconsidered, and that past efforts may bring present or future rewards. If badly placed, the Six of Cups could mean that the seeker lives too much in the past, or is too nostalgic and does not pay enough attention to present and future potentials.

Six of Swords

This card is an interesting combination of the harmony of the Number Six and the Swords, which so often indicate strife or difficulty. A ferryman carries a sorrowing woman and child across the water to a far shore. It is interesting to note that the water on the right-hand side of the boat is rough, while on the left it is calm. This indicates the moving away from difficulties towards more peaceful times. It can mean a literal journey, a move to a more pleasing environment; but this journey could also be on an inner level. This card can denote release of tension and anxiety after a period of strain, and a sense of harmony prevailing once again.

Six of Pentacles

The number of harmony is shown in this card by a merchant carefully weighing out gold to distribute fairly among the needy. This is a card which suggests that money owing will be paid; the seeker will receive what is rightfully his. There may be financial help from a generous friend or employer, and money affairs may

be put on a stable footing. There is also the suggestion that present prosperity should be shared with others.

The Sevens

Seven is the number of wisdom and the number relating to completion of cycles. There are seven personal planets in astrology, seven virtues, seven vices and seven deadly sins. On the seventh day, God rested. Inherent in this number is a sense of completion of a phase.

Seven of Wands

Six wands rise up to attack a young man, who fights on with courage. One of the attributes of the seven is deep purpose and valour, both of which are aptly depicted in this card. A successful change in profession is likely but strength and determination are necessary to achieve success. It could be that stiff competition will be met in business, but perseverance and courage will win out in the end. This card is also a card of knowledge and incorporates skills in teaching, lecturing or writing.

Seven of Cups

Fantastic visions arise out of seven cups floating in the clouds before a bewildered man. He does not know which to choose: the

castle, the jewels, the wreath of victory, the dragon or the curly-headed woman. In the centre, a draped figure represents his true self waiting to be unveiled. This card suggests that a choice has to be made, and much care and consideration needs to be devoted to it. One of the cups must be chosen and worked with, otherwise his dreams and ideas will remain castles in the clouds. It is a time in which the imagination works overtime and choices seem innumerable, so to choose one direction seems almost impossible. However, a choice must be made if anything is to be achieved. Accompanying the confusion over the decision is also an abundance of creative and artistic talent and energy.

Seven of Swords

A man appears to be escaping with a bundle of swords from a camp in the background. Two swords remain impaled behind him in the ground. He looks over his shoulder with a guilty expression. This card denotes the necessity for prudence and evasion in order to gain an objective – a time for brain not brawn. Direct or aggressive tactics will not be useful in this situation, but diplom-

acy and charm will. If the card is badly placed, a flight from a dishonourable act might be indicated.

Seven of Pentacles

A young farmer leans on his hoe and studies the vine he is cultivating. The seven days of his labour are finished yet he hesitates before accepting the harvest. There is a pause during the development of an enterprise or business. The young farmer in the card appears to be assessing what he has achieved and what needs to be done. He is a dreamer who has practical ideas and is working from a solid foundation. However, the card warns not to stop for long, for past efforts will only be successful through consistent effort.

The Eights

The Eight is the number of regeneration and balance of opposing forces. It betokens the death of the old, evil or wrong, and makes way for the new, pure and just. After all, a wise man dies a little every day in shedding old concepts, habits and ways of thinking as they become inappopriate.

Eight of Wands

Eight wands fly through the sky over peaceful lands below. This is a card denoting the need to be 'up and doing', a time for activities and new beginnings. It marks the end of a period of delay or stagnation, and indicates a time for initiative and action to begin. A busy exciting time ahead, suggesting travel and moves.

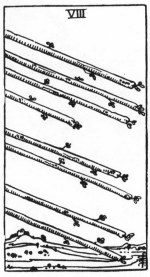

Eight of Cups

A man turns his back on eight neatly stacked cups, and heads towards a barren mountain. The care with which he collected and placed the cups shows his previous concern, but now he abandons them totally. The Moon, in both its full and waning quarters, looks on, signifying the end of something and the beginning of something new. The card indicates leaving the past behind, abandoning a situation through disappointment or disillusion.

Although a lot of care and investment has gone into building up a situation or relationship, it is not right, so the seeker has no choice but to abandon it in search of what is. Even though the cups behind are full, they cannot satisfy him.

Eight of Swords

A woman stands bound and blindfolded in what appears to be a marsh. Eight swords form a barrier around her and behind her in the distance, stands a castle built on bare rocks. A dismal-looking card in which the seeker is afraid of moving out of a situation which binds and restricts him. The restrictions are upon him through his own fear and indecision, but positively this card suggests that a sign will come to show him the way. The seeker must remain courageous as there are problems to overcome and important decisions to make. He will not remain paralysed by his own fears for ever.

Eight of Pentacles

An apprentice craftsman is carving out pentacles. He is happy and enthusiastic about his work, the fruits of which are proudly fastened to the block of wood beside him. This 'talent' card, allied with the energy of the eight, can indicate the possibility of turning a skill or talent into a profession, or money earned through such a skill. There is possible new employment in a skilled field although things are still in an apprentice stage. Hard work and practical ideas form the stable basis for building up a new and profitable career both in emotional and financial terms.

The Nines

In the Number Nine, all the forces of the other numbers are summed up and form a foundation, before completion which follows in the Ten.

Nine of Wands

A man stands ready as if to defend his territory. It is evident from his bandaged head that he has already fought; yet he is still willing and ready to fight again for what he holds dear. This is a card of strength and determination. It suggests that even when you feel as though you have come to the end of your fighting powers there is strength in reserve. It puts the seeker in a very strong position, and suggests victory through courage and endurance.

Nine of Cups

A well-dressed man sits with his arms crossed, nine upright cups forming an arch behind him. He looks well fed and contented, his

security both physically and emotionally is assured. This is the 'wish' card, signifying the fulfilment of a desire of paramount importance. Emotional stability is indicated as well as physical and material happiness. Sensual pleasure is also satisfied.

Nine of Swords

A sleepless woman sits up in bed, head in hands, seemingly in despair. Nine swords hang ominously overhead, the panel under her couch showing a picture of two swordsmen fighting. Her quilt

is decorated with the signs of the zodiac. This card suggests that the seeker senses impending doom and disaster, but the swords do not touch the woman and these fears may be unfounded. Often the fear of difficulties is worse than the reality and though there may be a difficult decision to be made or situation to face, the fear is far worse than the outcome.

Nine of Pentacles

A well-dressed woman stands alone in a flourishing vineyard. A falcon on her gloved hand indicates that her thoughts are well controlled. A manor house in the background denotes material well-being. This card often signifies one who is able to enjoy the good things in life, even though alone. The card suggests a solitary pleasure in physical comfort and material success, although it does not necessarily imply that the person is literally without relationships. It is more suggestive of one who is at peace within and therefore does not *need* constant companionship to feel contented. Material benefits are promised and appreciated.

The Tens

The meaning of the Ten is perfection through completion. Nine is commanded to be perfect in the Ten, the One of beginning placed next to the Zero of spirit, so the cycle which is completed in the Ten is then ready to return to One again. The Ten in the suits of the Minor Arcana shows the height of bliss and happiness in the Cups and Pentacles, while the Swords and Wands show trial and tribulation.

Ten of Wands

A man is shown carrying an impossibly heavy burden of ten wands shouldered in a very awkward and uncomfortable fashion. The burden seems more than he can bear yet he plods on towards the town in the distance. This card suggests that a burden is soon to be lifted, or a problem soon to be solved. However, the oppression is often self-imposed and much can be done by the seeker himself in order to relieve his load. The load can be physical, mental or emotional but something can be done to help lighten the weight.

Ten of Cups

A young couple stretch their arms forwards in gratitude towards the rainbow of promise. Two children dance before them and a comfortable home stands as a symbol of contentment behind them. This is the ultimate of what the Cups can bring in the way of love and happiness. A happy family life, inspired from above, is depicted with lasting contentment, contrasting with the sensual satisfaction and pleasure of the Nine. A lot of love is available both to give and to receive.

Ten of Swords

A figure lies face down in a desolate marshland. He is pierced by all ten swords and looks very dead. Beyond the lake, the dawn is breaking over the horizon. This card obviously signifies the end of something. It could be the end of a relationship, of a particular circumstance or of a false way of seeing a situation. It has a ring of truth and clarity of vision which brings about an inevitable death, while the dawn breaking in the distance once again heralds promise of rebirth. This grim-looking card has a positive sense of clearing the ground for something new.

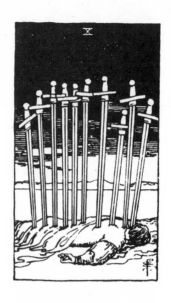

Ten of Pentacles

A richly-robed elderly gentleman, a grandfather perhaps, is seated in the foreground of the card. He is surrounded by his family, and

his dogs stand loyally by his knee. His castle and estate look well established and a sense of material security is well illustrated. This symbolizes financial stability and firm foundations for home and family life. It suggests property acquired for the founding of new generations, or traditions being passed down in the family with a feeling of continutiy and security. A materially settled way of life is indicated and selling or buying of property in favourable circumstances also comes under the influence of this card.

EXERCISES

At this stage I would like to suggest that you continue along the same line described in Part One. The exercises are vital in forming the core of your understanding of the Tarot images. Use the 'guided fantasy' exercises outlined previously for studying Justice, Temperance, Strength, The Hermit, The Wheel of Fortune and The Hanged Man. Take note of each image and record your feelings, thoughts and discoveries as you, on your journey through the Tarot, meet each card face to face. Note how they strike you, what you notice in particular, what impression or feeling you are left with as you move on, and so on.

Using the Minor Arcana, think of a description for each card which reminds you of a particular situation or feeling and note which cards stand out most noticeably and why.

PART THREE

DEATH
THE DEVIL
THE TOWER
THE STAR
THE MOON
THE SUN
JUDGEMENT
THE WORLD

THE PAGES
THE KNIGHTS
THE QUEENS
THE KINGS

Triumphant achievement

Success;
attainment;
symbol of
goals achieved;
completion
and reward

St Michael/Hermes:
guides Fool
out of
underworld
towards success
and
rejuvenation;

Apollo:
splendour
and triumph;
warmth;
light;
perception
and
directness

*Artemis/Demeter/
Hecate:*
sleep;
unconscious;
uncertainty;
fluctuation;
change

Star of Isis:
hope;
inspiration;
reawakening;
pool of memory
replenished
by star goddess

Divine
lightning;
harrowing
of Hell;
reborn of
divine fire

Pan:
purging
of worldly
identifications;
facing own
shadow and
darkness

Hades:
Fool must die
to be reborn;
stripping
of all
pretensions

DEATH

And now, the Fool must die.

The figure on the Death card enters menacingly as a skeleton wearing a suit of black armour. He rides a white horse and carries a black standard with a white rose upon it. A skull and crossbone pattern adorns the reins from the horse's bridle. Death rides over various people, uncaring for their rank or position. A king lies outstretched, crown fallen away; a bishop holds out his hand as if in prayer; a maiden kneeling turns aside her head as though she feels too young, too unprepared to face him. Only the small child appears unperturbed, even holding out a posy in welcome. Children do not fear change in the same way adults do. The background landscape shows a river flowing and two stone pillars with dawn breaking between them stand in the distance. The emphasis on black and white seems deliberate in this card, as white is the colour of purity and black is the colour of death. The two go hand-in-glove; for death purifies us, body, mind and spirit, and thus prepares us for rebirth. The scene illustrates the need to face death at some stage, in fact it comes to us all, at all ages, no matter how rich, how powerful, how beautiful or how young we may be. The river flowing across the card toward the sea represents the flow of life toward death. The river might be the Styx, the river which flows through the underworld filled with the waters of death, which are also transformable into life-giving waters of rebirth, or it might be the river of Jordan which Christian souls must cross to reach the promised land. The dawn breaking between the pillars of life and death suggests that within death is always the seed of life, for without death there could be no new life.

According to the legend, Dionysus was torn limb from limb by the Titans, who threw him into a cauldron and boiled away his flesh, leaving only his skeleton. This, in mythical terms, represents figuratively rather than actually what happens to the mind and heart of the Fool as he confronts Death. The Hanged Man is the first step towards the Fool's illumination when he consents to surrender his consciousness and make the journey into Hades.

Death strips him bare of all his pretensions before he is led naked into the presence of the underworld deities.

The Death card symbolizes change, the end of the old and the birth of the new. Life, both human and in nature, consists of constant cycles of death and renewal as the Fool first learned with the Empress. Each age of man has its phase, and each phase must end when it is lived out. After all, what parent would wish their child not to progress through infancy into childhood through adolescence into adulthood? It is the natural development both physically and psychologically in the life of man. Death marks the transition stages. Trees shed their leaves in autumn in order to prepare for the new growth in spring. The skeleton is like the bare trees, stripped of leaves to allow for new buds. The skeleton represents the stripping away of old outgrown feelings and thoughts – under the influence of Death, all is tried and tested and if to be found out-lived, must be discarded. Death can mean the end of things in many different ways. For instance, the Death card

DEATH.

could appear in the spread of someone about to be married, for it could signify the end of their single life, or in the spread of someone about to be divorced, as a symbol of the end of their marriage. Leaving school, leaving a job, leaving a country, all could be indicated by the appearance of the Death, but none of which signify *physical* death. The Death card in the Tarot is connected with transformation and change rather than death of the body. Feelings, emotions, thoughts and values undergo a transformation under the influence of Death, as the cycles which govern them end.

In a reading, this card heralds the inevitable ending of something, but with the promise of a new beginning. The pain that is suffered under the effect of Death is related to the willingness or unwillingness of the seeker to surrender to the inevitability of change.

THE DEVIL

The Fool's journey is now getting increasingly difficult. His travelling companions are stern, daunting characters, nowhere near as friendly and helpful as the figures he met at the outset of his travels. He has now been stripped of all worldly pretensions by Death and is led naked and trembling to meet the Devil himself.

The portrayal of the Devil figure is as interesting as it is menacing. The darkness of the card is immediately striking, as the black background enhances the central figure. The Devil himself, half-human, half-goat, stands upon a cube holding his right hand up while pointing a blazing torch to a naked couple who stand chained at his feet. The man and woman call to mind the couple in the Lovers card. They stand naked and vulnerable with weighty chains around their necks but their hands are free. They could lift the chains from their necks and set themselves free, or so it would seem. However, an added complication appears with the horns they have sprouted. This symbolizes that they have allowed themselves to become the Devil's disciples. They are chained to him by their thoughts as well as by their fear. In order to escape his bondage they must not only remove their chains but also radically alter their thoughts.

The image of the horned, hooved Devil originates with Pan, the goat-god of untamed nature and sexuality. He was worshipped by the Greeks as a life-giving fertility god, abundant and procreative. He represented natural energy in its chaotic and disordered state. Pan personified primitive, instinctive urges in man, particularly those of sexual energy. However, with the advent of Christianity, Pan was banished to hell and the devil is consequently often depicted with horns, hooves and a tail. Natural impulse and instinct was then frowned upon as evil, and man became ashamed to acknowlege his connection with such things.

The Devil teaches the Fool to recognize and accept all aspects of his nature, both dark and light. The Devil represents the blockage of repressed fears and feelings which, once removed, can release a great deal of positive energy. Energy in itself is neutral; it is how it is channelled that makes it positive or negative. The Devil points out that if our nature with both its aspects is not accepted, many inhibitions and phobias can accumulate unconsciously to prevent normal growth and development of the personality. In other words, the 'devil' in each of us must be faced, before we can come to terms with him and put his energy to good use. In Jungian terms the Devil represents the 'shadow', that part of our psyche we would rather ignore, the tiresome bit we see in everyone else but never in ourselves. As the Fool begins to accept his shadow, he is able to feel tolerance and compassion for himself and is in turn able to feel this towards others. Acceptance takes the place of blame, and he understands that all humans are composed of a combination of good and bad, light and shadow, and this understanding enables him to be human and accept his human limitations and failings.

In a reading, the Devil represents a message that blocks and inhibitions which hinder growth will be removed and carries the promise that if removed, great growth and progress is possible. 'Out of apparent evil, much good can come.'

THE DEVIL .

THE TOWER

The Fool now faces the lightning-struck Tower, the point at which he must split hell open and release himself from the darkness of his underworld journey. For the first time he encounters a card centring around a man-made image, the Tower. As such, it represents the external circumstances which constrict internal development; the social conventions which bind, and the society which governs, body, soul and mind. This card, like the Devil, has a dramatic black background, with the Tower itself perched precariously upon a high mountain peak. We can assume it is at a great height, for there is no visible vegetation nor evidence of man on the cliffs below. The clouds blowing past are even lower than the base of the Tower. A storm is in full spate; lightning flashes across the sky, striking the top of the Tower and causing damage. Flames flare out into the darkness, while two figures hurtle downwards from the windows, their faces contorted with fear as they fall headlong into the unknown. This imagery illustrates the shattering of the Fool's worldly illusions: the breaking down of false values and beliefs. Through his encounters with Death and the Devil, he has recognized inner conflicts, discovering as well the infinity of possibilities he has at his command: Death has stripped him of all pretensions, and the Devil has revealed the extent of his power. Now the Tower which encases false philosophies must be shattered. The walls of false beliefs and values must be torn down as the divine lightning penetrates the underworld of the unconscious to dispel the dark forces. The fork of lightning is the flash of illumination which splits hell open and breaks down existing forms to make way for the new.

Some old packs used the title *La Maison Dieu* which led some Tarot speculators to believe that this card depicted the Tower of Babel. However, older packs show that the word *Dieu* was in fact a corruption of the original word use, *Diefel*, meaning Devil, so the Tower, far from being the house of God, is actually the house of the Devil, or hell.

At this point, the Fool must sort out for himself which way is right for him. It is the point at which he abandons whatever is not truly his own. It is often the case that, for years, we live as we have been taught, even though what may have suited those who taught us might not suit us. There comes a time when our needs, thoughts and ideas need to be tested, evaluated and lived by. The conflicts inherent in our behaviour when we attempt to structure our lives by convention are symbolized by the Tower, a narrow, constricting edifice, and the lightning represents the flash of vision which causes us to change and live our own chosen way.

In a layout, this card denotes the necessary breaking down of existing forms to make way for new. New life and new ways are indicated; rigid or imprisoning structures need to be torn down and replaced. This card stands for the defeat of false philosophies and the triumph of true ones.

THE TOWER.

THE STAR

At last the time for renewal is nigh! After the sombre underworld, the shining promise of the Star refreshes and renews the Fool's drooping spirits. At last we are back to brightly coloured images like those encountered by the Fool when he began his travels. A feeling of release comes upon him as he meets the beautiful Star image. A maiden is kneeling, naked, pouring water from two pitchers, one into the pool as if to replenish it and the other over the green earth as if to refresh it. The steady flow of water on to the land divides into five streams. In the background a bird perches in a tree. The nudity of the maiden represents truth unveiled; she has no need of protective garments for she has nothing to fear and nothing to hide. She is young, for she stands for renewal. The pool she kneels besides might be the Pool of Memory, which, although situated in the twilight realm of the underworld, has its water replenished by Mnemosyne, goddess of memory. The Fool drinks of these waters so as not to forget his underworld experience. The five streams of water stand for the five senses, and the bird represents the Ibis of immortality, sacred bird of Thoth, god of all arts. The bird is a symbol of the spirit's ability to rise to high levels of emotional and spiritual consciousness. The Star has always been an emblem of hope and promise; a light to steer by. The wise men followed the bright star to Bethlehem; astrologers gain knowledge through charting the movement of the heavenly bodies; mariners use the stars to set their ships' courses. Even popular songs tell us that if you wish upon a star, your dreams come true.

The Tarot Star may be connected with the Star of Isis, goddess of Egypt. During the dry season in Egypt, the land became parched and barren, so that even the great river Nile would shrink dramatically. The people would fear starvation until the longed for Star of Isis would appear and herald the coming of rain to replenish the river and put new life back into the dead lands. The people of Egypt rejoiced and were filled with awe of the 'magic of Isis'.

Each man needs a goal, an aim towards which to strive. We all

107

need faith, and the belief that our hopes and wishes will be fulfilled, that our dreams *will* come true. The Star is symbolic of that faith, that hope. Without the inspiration of the Star, life would become dull and lack-lustre. The Star provides that little bit of magic which spurs us on and keeps us going in times of stress and doubt. The faith that things can improve is essential in difficult times, and the Star is that emblem of the inner light which guides us.

In a reading, the Star is a happy message of promise, good fortune, optimism and joy. It suggests inspiration, a sense of purpose and the renewal of life's forces and energy.

THE MOON

As the Fool's journey reaches its final stages, he realizes that there is still much to learn. After the dark sequence of cards in the underworld, he experienced a brief, but glorious respite with the Star, only to discover that the next card, the Moon, is another sombre one. At first glance, this card seems similar to the Star, but on closer examination it is not as calm as it appears. The land-scape – the pool and green meadows backed by distant mountains – is not dissimilar to the Star's setting. It is still country of imagination. Here, however, there is no human figure to relate to, only the faces of the Moon. The pool, in the forefront of the card, is disturbed by a crayfish crawling out; two animals, a dog and a wolf, appear to be baying at the Moon. A road leads towards twin pillars. The crayfish is symbolic of innermost fears forcing their way to the surface of consciousness. The crayfish might represent childhood fears reappearing in adult life, still managing to cause fear and anxiety even though we may recognize the lack of logic in this. As the crayfish crawls into consciousness we often try to push him back, where he continues to exist, giving rise to vague fears and unacknowledged anxieties until such time as we allow the crayfish, or our fears, to come right out of the pool of the uncon-scious and be faced. The pool might be the Pool of Forgetfulness, which lies to the left of the Pool of Memory in the dark world of Hades. We try to forget that which gives rise to unpleasant or uncomfortable feelings or memories but the crayfish periodically reminds us of them by struggling out of the water. The other animals in the image, the dog and wolf, are both creatures of the underworld, guides of souls to the land of the dead. These animals are sacred to Hecate, goddess of the dark moon and enchantment and the infernal regions. The idea of dogs and wolves baying at the full moon is a powerful image suggesting madness or lunacy. The road, however, leads through the two pillars, as a suggestion of movement between conscious and unconscious.

The Moon shines down upon the scene, revealing her three faces: new, full and old, which correspond to the faces of woman: virgin, mother and hag. Mythically, each face can be compared to a goddess; Artemis, the virgin moon goddess for the new moon; Demeter, the earth mother goddess, for the full moon; Hecate, witch-enchantress goddess for the dark face of the moon. The three faces reveal the three aspects of femininity: the virgin, full of potential waiting to be fulfilled; the mother, potential fulfilled; the hag, potential shrivelled up or wasted.

The Moon is the mistress of the night, the womb to which men return each night to rest, sleep and dream. The Moon was once thought of as the home of the dead, for it was believed that the dying would leave their bodies and be drawn up to the moon where they would be kept safe until time was ripe for rebirth. The Moon was thus seen as the womb which gave forth new life as well as taking it away. She was worshipped as the great mother from whom all life sprang and to whom all life returned. The Moon rules the waxing and waning rhythms of life, of tides and all natural cycles. The Moon also symbolizes feelings and emotions which are by nature volatile, nebulous and uncertain. She rules the realm of unconscious thought, dream and fantasy, and as the High Priestess signified the wisdom of the unconscious revealed in a controlled way, the Moon symbolizes the unconscious in its unpredictable and uncontrolled aspects. These aspects need to be

THE MOON.

transformed into wisdom but if they are all able to function together harmoniously they can form part of the well-integrated personality.

In a reading, the Moon usually points to a phase of fluctuation and change. It often indicates uncertainty and even illusion. It can also suggest that solutions to problems can be found through dreams and intuitions rather than logic and reason.

THE SUN

Once again, after darkness there is light. The Sun is a cheerful and welcome image after the misty uncertainty of the Moon. A naked child riding a white horse, joyfully waves a bright red banner. In the background, sunflowers group along a wall and an enormous Sun shines rays which are alternately straight and wavy. The child stretches out his arms in a gesture of joy and friendship, his face radiant. The Sun's image of a naked child represents greeting of the Fool's new-found state of optimism with joy. The image of a child, rather than an adult figure, points towards the chance the Fool has to grow up again; he has the opportunity to revert to a childlike state so he can restart his inner or spiritual growth. The white horse is the same one as that ridden by Death, while red is the colour of desire and energy. The banner is symbolic of all the cloaks worn by the earlier Trumps, cast off, waved in the air with triumph and celebration. Their lessons have been learned. The straight and wavy rays of the Sun indicate the dual nature of the card, both its positive and negative aspects. The wall in the background represents the formation of the Fool's past life and his limitations. It represents all he has learned and done so far; the grey pattern of experience, a solid foundation from which he can now ride forward.

The Sun has many mythical associations and an obvious one is the Greek sun god, Apollo. He was the god of light, born of Leto, goddess of night, and his shrine, the oracle at Delphi, was sacred to all goddesses of darkness. Apollo's twin sister was Artemis, the Moon goddess. Apollo was an archer god whose fiery arrows could heal sickness but could also bring sudden death to those who ran foul of him. He was often depicted with his famous lyre as the god of music, poetry and song. He was a god of form, shaping elusive aspects of the psyche into durable and permanent expression, often as an artistic nature.

The Sun symbolizes the masculine capacity to impart form and structure. His influence gives form to the formless, shape to the shapeless. The Sun god presides over the arts as well as over the activity of the intellect; man's rational capacity to impose order and coherence on the fluctuating moods of his experience. The Sun is a card of daylight, which, while it lasts, is a time for vigorous activity and clear perception. In this respect, the Sun complements the Moon; for if the Moon represents the unconscious in its murky darkness, the Sun is consciousness in all its bright lucidity. If the Moon represents the feeling nature, the Sun stands for the capacity for thought. And as the Moon is formless, so the Sun is form.

The Sun, like the Moon, has its negative aspects. While form, structure, expression and articulation are things which can prove a great advantage, there are circumstances when they can be taken too far. It can be a mistake, for example, to structure and regulate feelings in accordance with logic. The sun can ripen fruit but can also lay waste a desert. Apollo's fiery arrows, as the Sun's warm rays, can heal or kill. However, if the Fool approaches the Sun with reverence and caution he can richly benefit from this benevolent source of life and strength.

In a spread, the card represents energy and a source of strength. The Sun stands for success, prosperity, happiness and true friends. It seems to brighten all the cards surrounding it, adding a sense of optimism and good cheer.

THE SUN .

JUDGEMENT

Judgement is the penultimate stage of the Fool's journey. He has almost reached his goal with only two more cards to encounter. The Judgement card depicts an angel appearing from the clouds, a halo of golden hair around his young face. He is blowing a mighty trumpet from which hangs a white banner emblazoned with a red cross. Three naked figures arise from coffins stretching out their arms, as do other figures in the distance. The points of the cross denote the way to spiritual ascent is through the reconciliation of opposites to form a higher unity, and the central crossing point of the two lines shows a joining together of all things that have been separate or separated. The naked figures illustrate more important symbolic detail. They are naked because they have thrown off their garments of worldliness in favour of spirituality. The figures appear to be rising from their graves: the coffins are open and they are free to climb out. The blackness of the tomb represents the dark underworld, life without initiation. The figures have undergone a spiritual rebirth; they died in order to find themselves and to acquire new life to which they are now being summoned.

The angel blowing the trumpet could be St Michael, who functions as a guide of souls and whose trumpet rings out at the Day of Judgement. Michael was one of the seven archangels who was said to guide the planets, his own special planet being Mercury. This brings us back full circle to Hermes, known to the Romans as Mercury, the guide of souls whom the Fool first met at the beginning of his journey under the guise of the Magician. The Magician led the Fool unseen along the way and now leads him triumphantly towards his goal.

As its image suggests, Judgement is a card of summing-up, of balancing accounts; through this card the Fool's progress is evaluated and assessed. Judgement may symbolize what in Eastern thought is called Karma, the principle whereby man's actions produce their appropriate reward or punishment, which in Western tradition is summed up by the phrase, 'as you sow, so shall you reap'. Judgement reflects a process of self-appraisal, an honest and sincere attempt to come to terms with oneself and whatever resolutions one has found for inner conflict. It necessitates removing the veils through which man generally perceives himself and either over-estimates or under-estimates his efforts. Excessive modesty or self-recrimination is just as erroneous as excessive egotism or complacency. Judgement stresses the need to evaluate oneself and one's accomplishments at their true worth and though we condemn those who puff themselves up, we should also condemn those who, for whatever reason, sell themselves short.

The card of Judgement marks the completion of the karmic cycle, in which reward or penalties are conferred in accordance with one's true worth.

In a reading, the card signifies the final settlement of a matter, a 'clean slate' – paying off old debts and a preparedness for the resurrection of a new beginning. It indicates that things which have lain fallow will come to life, and reward for past effort will finally be forthcoming. It is a time for rejoicing and renewal.

JUDGEMENT.

THE WORLD

At last we have arrived at the World, the final and most complex card in the Major Trumps. The image portrays a dancing figure draped in a purple sash. The figure is dancing in a wreath of laurel, carrying a wand in each hand. The four corners of the card reveal the heads of a lion, an eagle, a man and a bull. The purple sash that the World dancer wears is the colour of wisdom and divinity and is draped in such a way as to conceal the sexual gender, for this figure represents a hermaphrodite, a symbol of unity between the sexes. The two wands represent the duality the Fool had encountered so many times along his route. There has been constant emphasis on two halves forming a whole; pairs and opposites combining to become one. The wreath of laurel leaves is a symbol of success and triumph. The four heads at the compass points stand for the fixed zodiacal signs and reflect the four seasons and elements: Lion—Leo—Summer—Fire; Eagle—Scorpio—Autumn—Water; Man—Aquarius—Winter—Air; Bull—Taurus—Spring—Earth. The World dancer is seemingly blending and unifying the opposites to create harmony and balance as though the four elements have been combined to create a fifth complete one. The oval wreath can also symbolize the womb, and the dancer, the foetus, waiting to be born again as the Fool, so the procession of Trumps may begin again.

This card symbolizes completeness by showing oneness with self and nature. It represents an establishment of oneself in one's rightful place, in relation to the cosmos and as an expression of internal and external harmony. The individual is now at one with nature and the world; there is a sense of satisfaction and achievement at finding one's rightful place. Realization of the World is the objective to which mystics have aspired from time immemorial. Jung calls it Realization of The Archetype of The Self; Christianity calls it Beatitude; it is the supreme goal in Buddhist, Hindu and Taoist traditions as well as the goal to which the cabalist aspires. It involves the supreme integration of self and the cosmos as well as unity, harmony and balance. Whether it is a viable expectation for the average individual is questionable but certainly intimations of it can be offered. The main point is that the Tarot links up at this stage with something much vaster than simply divination. Here the Tarot connects with the great mystic traditions which have constituted a common denominator between all the world's great religions and systems of philosophical thought from ancient times up to the present day.

THE WORLD.

In readings, however, this card shows the completion of one phase or stage of life; it promises success, harmony and triumphant achievement. It is the realization of a sought after prize or goal.

The Court Cards

We now come to the final section of the Minor Arcana, namely the Court cards. They act as a link or bridge between the Major and Minor and are often quite difficult to interpret because they can symbolize a number of different things. For example, they could symbolize a particular type of person entering the seeker's life; they could represent an aspect of the seeker's own personality or they could indicate an actual event. This obviously makes it difficult to decide how to read the Court cards and there are no hard-and-fast rules. To a large extent, practice and experience will help, as well as looking at the overall layout of the cards and the seeker's question or situation. As always, the more feeling each card holds for you, the easier it will become to know how to interpret it in each particular case. Some people find that linking the Court cards with astrological signs gives a fuller impression of each figure's personality, so where appropriate I have included my own associations.

The Pages

The Pages are cards which represent children, or an aspect of personality just beginning to develop. If they symbolize an event it is usually the beginning of something new and undeveloped. As with Aces to Tens, the elements reflect the basic energy of the Pages differently through each suit.

The Page of Wands

Two symbols recur through the Wand Court cards, that of the lion and the salamander. Both are fiery creatures; the lion is Leo's

PAGE of WANDS.

symbol, the salamander was a legendary lizard believed to live in the flames of fire. The Page of Wands wears a tunic covered in salamanders and stands in a scorching desert. Yellow and orange are the warm fiery colours which dominate this suit's images. The Page stands proudly holding his sturdy Wand and, though small, he gives an air of strength and determination. If he stands for a child or young person in a spread, he may symbolize a quick, intuitive, enthusiastic personality. His daring and energy could associate him with Aries, the first fire sign of the zodiac which heralds the coming of Spring. Aries is a sign full of new life and vitality as is the Page of Wands. If the seeker is trying to develop qualities of enthusiasm and optimism within him or herself, this card can be a helpful one. In terms of representing an event, the Page may be a bearer of good news, glad tidings, a desire for growth and knowledge along with the opportunity to achieve this.

The Page of Cups

The two themes which run through the suit of Cups are the fish and water. The fish is a symbol of creative imagination and water

PAGE of CUPS.

represents the feelings and the unconscious mind. The colours of the Cups are soft pink and blue; the imagery and colours reflect sweetness and gentleness, characteristic of this suit. The Page of Cups gazes dreamily at the cup in his hand as a fish emerges from it, symbolizing the birth of creative imagination and new life. If the Page in a spread is indicative of a young person, he stands for a sensitive, kind natured, feeling type with strong artistic or even psychic talents, often connected with the watery sign of Cancer. The Page of Cups can indicate these qualities, in embryo, in the seeker. He may bring news of a birth, perhaps the birth of a child or of new feelings and attitudes. For example, if a seeker had been hurt or was afraid to let go emotionally, this card could indicate the fragile new beginnings in starting to trust again.

The Page of Swords

The images which dominate the suit of Swords are airy ones: clouds, birds and butterflies. Blue and purple are the colours which run through the suit's images and although purple is the colour for wisdom and justice, it is not softened with much

PAGE of SWORDS.

warmth, for the blue is icy cold. The Page of Swords stands on guard, as if ready to defend himself. He is brandishing a sword above his head, checking over his shoulder for fear of attack from behind. If he represents a young person, it could be a ruthless character, very clever but unconcerned about the feelings of others. He is not malicious on purpose, but if anyone gets in his way he will simply trample them underfoot. The Page of Swords indicates one who has an extremely strong will and who is rather cold and calculating. He may stand for a spy or deceitful person not to be trusted. In an event, he might stand for situations complicated by rumour-spreading or gossip mongering.

The Page of Pentacles

Golden skies and indications of nature's rich bounty seem to be the main themes of the Pentacle suit. The Page is pictured standing in a lush field dotted with little flowers, gazing intently at the golden pentacle he holds carefully in his hand. He is dressed in the colours of the suit, green and brown, colours of the earth. The suit of Pentacles is associated primarily with earthly possessions and this Page indicates a child or young person who has respect for

PAGE of PENTACLES.

material things and takes the learning of new ideas seriously. He is careful, hard-working and diligent, though sometimes rather solemn. The Page of Pentacles could be associated with the meticulous sign of Virgo. If the seeker is trying to develop a sense of material value, or start a new business venture, this is a good card. As an event, the Page of Pentacles often signifies an opportunity to make money, usually starting from the bottom but with plenty of promise for the future.

The Knights

We now come to the Knights, the cards which symbolize movement and action. The Knights stand for youth, though not as young as the Pages, and they are all seekers, searching through desert, ocean, sky or field to reach their chosen goal.

The Knight of Wands

A handsome knight on a fine steed, gallops across desert-like terrain. He is wearing a tunic embroidered with salamanders over

KNIGHT of WANDS.

his suit of armour. The Knight of Wands has an air of purpose and confidence about him, as he holds the reins of his horse casually in one hand and a wand, symbol of creative energy, in the other. This young man has splendid ideas and a fine sense of adventure; he makes a generous and warm friend or lover, although he is unpredictable and hasty in judgement. He has a good sense of humour and will do anything for fun. If he stands for an event, it is usually a change of residence or a long journey, even immigration.

The Knight of Cups

The Knight of Cups, although as handsome as the Knight of Wands, proceeds on his way in a much gentler fashion. His

KNIGHT of CUPS.

beautiful white horse bows its head coyly, moving slowly and deliberately, unlike the confident gallop of the Knight of Wands. A stream runs through the land, dividing the hills and valley, which suggests the thin divide between the conscious and the unconscious. The Knight of Cups wears a winged helmet which represents his spiritual aspirations, and his tunic is decorated with the fish of creative imagination. He stands for a refined, artistic, high-principled youth, an idealist and seeker of perfection. He is like the knights of the Holy Grail; he shares their quest for truth, beauty and love, and nothing will deter him from this search. If he stands for an event, it is often a proposal of marriage, or a proposition in the field of art, or even a rival in love.

The Knight of Swords

The Knight of Swords dashes across the card, his horse's legs outstretched, its mane flying in the wind. The emphasis is on speed; the swift action of the wind is pictured often in this suit. In the background of the card, the wind has bent the cypress trees which are the trees of sorrow or strife. The Knight leans forward in his seat, his sword poised for battle.

The Knight of Swords is a curious mixture, for he has an attractive, magnetic personality and easily draws attention and affection from others, but he seems to have no need of them. He has a ruthless quality and, although not intentionally cruel, he may often hurt others while he selfishly pursues his own ends. He is not emotionally supportive because it does not occur to him to

KNIGHT of SWORDS .

be. However, he does have a brilliant mind and good business judgement, and he gets on well in his career. As an event, he represents a situation which is very swiftly started amid great excitement, and dies down almost as quickly leaving a certain amount of chaos in its wake.

The Knight of Pentacles

The Knight of Pentacles is most noticeably different from the other three in that his horse stands quite still. The Knight and his steed are depicted in a freshly ploughed field, quietly contemplating their surroundings. The image is a peaceful one and this Knight is a peaceful, gentle fellow with infinite patience and tolerance. He is kind and trustworthy and will carry out a task to completion, no matter how long it may take. He always reaches his goal because he never gives up and always sets his sights on achievable rewards. In this he is unlike the Knight of Wands, who often gets waylaid by something interesting or fun; the Knight of Cups, whose goals are so idealistic they can almost never be reached; or the Knight of Swords, who is sometimes too impatient to wait for things to come to fruition. The Knight of Pentacles

KNIGHT of PENTACLES.

plods on without frenzy or excitement, but his plodding wins him the rewards. He is kind to animals and children and loves all things pertaining to nature. He indicates just such a person, unadventurous but utterly reliable. His qualities of perseverence and capacity for honest hard work are often sought by others. As an event, he stands for the eventual positive outcome of a situation which has dragged on for a long while, or which has appeared fruitless.

The Queens

In layouts, the Queens can be taken for actual people or parts of the seeker's personality, but they do not tend to indicate events in the way that the Pages and Knights can.

The Queen of Wands

A noble-looking woman, proud and tall, is seated upon a throne adorned with the fiery emblem of lions. She carries a sunflower in her left hand; in her right, she bears a wand, symbol of her queenly

authority. At her feet sits a black cat, denoting her role as 'queen of hearth and home'. This Queen is full of the love of life; she can successfully run a home and family but still finds time and energy to vigorously pursue her own interests. She can have several projects going at one time yet never lets anything detract from the energy she puts into her home life. She is well-liked and will always help her friends enthusiastically, but if crossed she fights as fiercely as any lioness. Her tireless versatility is a quality often sought after.

The Queen of Cups

A very different Queen, indeed, to the vibrant Queen of Wands. The dreamy, fey Queen of Cups sits upon an elaborate throne decorated with baby mermaids. Her flowing dress mingles with the water lapping at her feet and she gazes trance-like into an ornate cup, its handles shaped like angels. The cup has a lid on it which suggests that her thoughts are in the realm of the uncon- scious. The Queen of emotions is a person who has reached a degree of understanding of her own emotional depth and lives to a large extent in the realm of fantasy and imagination. The Queen

QUEEN of CUPS.

of Cups is often the object of the love of others attracting admiration for her qualities of gentleness and sensitivity, yet she has a certain air of containedness which makes her quite fascinating. She is highly artistic and creative, even mystical or prophetic. However, she is deeply involved in her inner world that it makes relationships of an everyday nature strangely difficult for her. The Queen of Cups has qualities which are often sought after by those who need to pay attention to their inner worlds as well as their outer ones.

The Queen of Swords

The Queen of Swords is a sombre figure, seated upright on a throne decorated with a winged angel and butterflies. Storm clouds gather in the darkening sky, her cloak is patterned with little clouds. She holds her sword straight and her face is solemn yet resigned. The Queen of Swords represents a woman who has experienced sorrow, who may be alone through widowhood, divorce or separation. She has loved and lost but will love again; she must bear her pain silently and with courage. The Queen of Swords is a symbol of strong will and determination, a woman

QUEEN of SWORDS.

who can bear whatever life presents her with. She waits out her time of mourning patiently, knowing, like Cronus, that her Golden Age will return. Acquiring this Queen's qualities to bear suffering with strength can be supportive and helpful in times of loss and sorrow.

The Queen of Pentacles

The Queen of Pentacles sits contentedly in fertile fields, her throne rich with the fruits of the earth. The head of a goat, symbol of earthy Capricorn, forms her arm-rest. The card is framed with flowers and a rabbit, symbol of fertility, stands in one corner. The Queen of Pentacles is practical and materialistic. She loves the good things in life and, having acquired them, is then easily content to spend her life enjoying them. She knows what she wants and is satisfied when she gets it. She accepts responsibilities gladly and is fair and wise in business. This Queen is often rich because she works hard for material gain. She can indicate a helpful friend or employer, because she is generous with her good fortune and may indicate help given of a practical nature.

The Kings

The Kings, as partners to the Queens, stand for men, and, like the Queens, they stand for authority within their own suits.

The King of Wands

The King of Wands sits forward restlessly, looking set for action. As a fiery king, his throne and robes are adorned with images of lions and salamanders. A live salamander stands beside him, also looking poised for action. This King is a master of wit and charm. He is warm and generous with a good sense of humour and a strong liking for fun. He could persuade anyone into anything, could even 'sell ice to eskimos', because he is so amusing and optimistic. The King of Wands is full of new ideas and has an abundance of vision and foresight. His 'hunches' always seem to pay off and he will happily make instant decisions, even on major matters. However, he dislikes detail and gets easily irritated if his enthusiasm or optimism is curbed by the practicalities or realities of life. He has total trust in his world of ideas and intuition, riding

KING of WANDS

on the crest of the waves of success, and forgetting any venture which fails.

The King of Cups

The King of Cups sits on a throne in troubled seas. A fish, symbol of creative imagination, leaps over the waves far in the distance, but the golden fish around the King's neck seems an empty token compared to the lively imagination which lies behind him. His feet do not touch the water; he seems stiff and uncomfortable, unlike his Queen who merges into the waves without effort. He is the master of emotions, and can change his moods at will, but there is a feeling about the King of Cups which suggests that he is not really connected with his element. Masculinity often symbolizes conscious thought and intellect and is therefore not totally at ease in the realms of deep emotion. This King is often to be found in the helping professions because of his desire to be united with his unconscious world which does not come easily to him. He tends to pay lip-service to feelings rather than merging with them. If the King of Cups comes up in a spread representing an aspect of a

KING of CUPS.

seeker's personality, it might mean that it is time for him to get truly in touch with his feelings.

The King of Swords

The King of Swords stares straight ahead, his sword upright. Storm clouds, a familiar sight in the Swords suit now, gather in the sky, but the air looks still. The cypress trees stand straight and unruffled by wind. The King himself looks calm and self-assured, wearing a purple cloak, the colour of wisdom. He gives the impression of inner strength and conviction. The Swords, being the suit of air and the mind, emphasize a love of truth and justice. This King is one who rules with justice, and firm moral convictions, and is deeply committed, both in friendship and in enmity. He is not easily swayed by pleas for mercy or compassion; he judges harshly but with scrupulous fairness. He is often found in positions of authority and is a figure much feared but always respected. He can be suspicious and over-cautious, the 'strong silent type'. His qualities of strength of character, a sense of fairness and justice, are highly commendable as long as they can be tempered with a little compassion.

KING of SWORDS.

The King of Pentacles

The King of Pentacles is surrounded by riches, his lavish throne adorned with a bull's head, symbol of Taurus, the sign denoting love of material possessions. His robes are decorated with bunches of grapes and his crown with red roses. Beyond stands a fine castle symbolizing his earthly achievements. He is a man who loves money and riches and is happy to amass as much as possible. He is very clever in business matters, a bit of a financial wizard. It seems as though he only has to touch a deal for it to turn to gold, a bit like King Midas. However, he is not corrupt in his love of riches and earns money through hard, patient effort, not through unworthy or dishonest business dealings. He is generous with what he has and gladly shares the fruits of his labour with others. The quality of being content with what you have is fairly uncommon and this simple lesson, so hard to learn, can be taught by the King of Pentacles.

EXERCISES

Now that you have completed your detailed examination of the whole pack, finish off the guided fantasy exercises for the remaining Major Arcana, using the same procedure as in Parts One and Two. You will, therefore, be starting with Death and working through each card in turn: the Devil; the Tower; the Star; the Moon; the Sun; Judgement and the World. Take note of your feelings about each meeting with the image or figure on the card. Remember that the crucial part of this exercise is allowing yourself enough time to relax thoroughly and pay attention to each character you meet. Lastly, think about yourself as the Fool, having finally completed your journey through the Major Trumps. Compare your notes and feelings to the first exercise, when you imagined yourself at the beginning of the journey. How have you changed? What have you learned? and so on.

The next exercise is a good one to test your knowledge and progress in learning the cards and their meanings. Spread the whole pack down in front of you and pick out a number of cards at random. Turn them up and write down all the detail and divinatory meanings you can think of, before checking back through the text to see how much you were able to remember spontaneously.

Now take the Court cards and look at each in turn. Try to imagine the personality of each; see which character is like you or not like you; see if any personality reminds you of a friend, family member or colleague. Try to connect each card with a personal association. If you like, make up little stories about the various suits or 'families'. It is all helpful in getting to know your cards as intimately as possible.

Once you feel really comfortable with the images, their meanings and messages, you are ready for the fourth and final part: mastering the art of interpretation.

PART FOUR
Readings

You are now ready to move on to the final section in which some sample spreads can be examined. It is a good idea to experiment with as many different layouts as you like until you find the format which suits you best. Please do not think that the spreads illustrated here are the only ones available. There are a great many to choose from, or, if you like, you can make up your own spreads. The actual 'layout' means the various positions in which the cards are laid out, each relating to specific areas of life, such as relationships, work, etc. This gives a framework within which to work and gives the reading a loose structure. The question of who shuffles the cards, the reader or seeker, is another of personal preference. Some readers hand the deck of cards to the seeker to shuffle and then deal the cards off the top of the pack. Others, myself included, prefer to do all the shuffling themselves and simply invite the seeker to select a certain number of cards from the pack which is spread face-down before them.

Again, as a personal preference, I use the Major and Minor Arcana separately for a couple of spreads and then mix them together for the final reading. I use the Minor Arcana for the 'Celtic Cross' reading (see page 140) to gain a picture of the seeker's position in life in terms of career, relationships, trials, etc., and then go in greater depth to find a reflection of the seeker's inner life using the Major Arcana 'Star' (see page 144) spread, also figured below. I then use either the 5-card Horseshoe spread (see page 137) or the Tree of Life reading (see page 148), if I need more detail, using the Major and Minor Arcana mixed together. Once again, while I can only illustrate my own preferred method of reading, it is up to you to experiment until you find the way that suits you best.

At this point, it may be useful to re-emphasize the main objectives when reading the Tarot. As has already been stated, many seekers will consult the Tarot when they are in a confused or unhappy state or when they are facing a difficult decision or situation. They come expecting and hoping for help or guidance but at the same time often hold a notion that 'nothing should be revealed to the reader' in case it 'helps' in translating the sequence of cards more accurately. This attitude can be rather counter-productive for while the cards will reflect the situation they cannot pin-point minute detail, so shared comment and dialogue can be very profitable. The Tarot is not a fortune-telling computer; it is a method whereby the reader can contact unconscious knowledge, be fed clues to forthcoming events and thus might be able to offer some guidance.

Seekers are often concerned about whether their readings will be 'good' or 'bad'. It is not possible to equate the Tarot with such morally concrete statements; the Tarot does not lay down such value judgements. What it does do is offer an understanding of the situation the seeker is in and the most constructive way to handle the energies, whether 'difficult' or 'easy'. Let's take an example: if Death comes up in a reading the seeker might panic, assuming that they or someone close to them is about to die, in which case you could reassure them that this card does not mean physical death, while encouraging them to look at the aspect of themselves or their lives which has ended its usefulness. The opportunity for new life that Death brings is to be welcomed although the period of mourning the loss may be a sad one. Suppose the Devil appears in a spread, another card popularly believed to be 'bad', you could point out the possibilities the Devil indicates for bringing unconscious blocks or inhibitions which prevent growth, to consciousness. The Devil stands for a positive opportunity to release such constraints, even though it may be painful in the process.

A useful question you can put to yourself when approaching the cards is 'what is the best course of action indicated by these cards for this person at this time?'

Let us now look at some actual spreads, using layouts for seekers who have kindly given me permission to use their readings and case-histories, although their names have been changed. I deliberately chose some readings which have the same cards in common, to show how each card can work differently in each spread, which in turn reflects the seeker's particular set of life circumstances.

1. The·5-Card Horseshoe

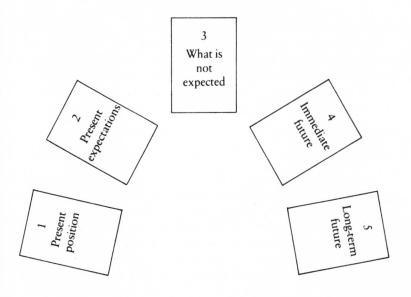

Sally-Ann

The first reading we are examining is for Sally-Ann, a young woman aged twenty-seven, single and living in a shared flat with another girl. She came to see me for a reading because she faced a dilemma in her priorities. Should she put her boyfriend or her career prospects first? For some time she had been trying to get a small business of her own underway, rather unsuccessfully, but had recently met a man with whom she was becoming increasingly involved. She was unsure whether to put her work, which had been important for such a long time, first, or whether to abandon the business project in favour of devoting more time and energy to her new relationship. She did not feel she had enough energy to do both, and felt confused and miserable about it.

Card one, 4 of Cups: present position

The 4 of Cups represents Sally-Ann's present position, her current feelings and surroundings. This card shows a young man staring discontentedly at three full cups before him and being offered opportunities from the clouds with the fourth, yet he cannot seem to accept them. Sally-Ann seems to be in a state of depression and confusion despite the fact that her situation is offering her a great deal. The 4 of Cups indicates the lack of ability to choose, and although she has potentially a lot of energy, none of it seems to be channelled in a positive direction.

Card two, 2 of Swords: present expectations

The second card drawn is the 2 of Swords, which represents what Sally-Ann currently expects. The image on this card shows a blindfolded woman, carefully balancing two heavy swords above her head. From this we can see that Sally-Ann is unable to face up to what her real desires are. She is afraid to look at what she really wants or feels (the water behind being the sea of her emotions) for she knows that that will entail making a decision (the rocks jutting above the water represent hard facts) which she feels too uncertain to face.

Card three, 4 of Pentacles: what is not expected

The third card, the 4 of Pentacles, shows what she does not expect. This card symbolizes a fear of letting go of what has been carefully acquired. It seems that Sally-Ann did not expect her inner feelings to be so fearful of letting her freedom go, in order to commit herself to her boyfriend, or to give up the chance of making a go of her business. As she was unconscious of this aspect of the situation, this insight gave her food for thought. She had not realized how much she wanted to hang on to everything as it was, even though it was preventing growth and development. Because she felt so reluctant to take any risks it made it impossible for her to change or gain anything, so the closed atmosphere of this card linked up with the two previous cards: nothing ventured, nothing gained. In trying to keep everything as it was, she was actually preventing movement, which was why she felt so depressed and stuck.

Card four, 5 of Swords: immediate future

The fourth card, the 5 of Swords, indicated the short-term future influences. This card seemed to suggest that it would be sensible for Sally-Ann to give up the present struggle, which was getting her nowhere, and to realize that she was actually tackling something too big for her. We both felt this applied to her trying to start up a business which had so far proved an expensive failure. Sally-Ann felt the message of this card was that she should stop banging her head against a brick wall businesswise and try another route. This card is one which suggests accepting limitations and acknowledging defeat before moving on to something more profitable and feasible.

Card five, Ace of Cups: long-term future

The last card to be drawn in this particular spread was the Ace of Cups. This card showed her long-term future filled with an abundance of love and happiness. It certainly seemed to indicate some light at the end of this tunnel and showed that a strong loving union could provide strength and direction.

I heard from Sally-Ann some eight months after this reading and she told me that she had given up her business, had bought a flat with her boyfriend and was working in a company which provided her with an interesting and stimulating job. The relationship was working out well and she said that by giving up one thing she had gained a great deal.

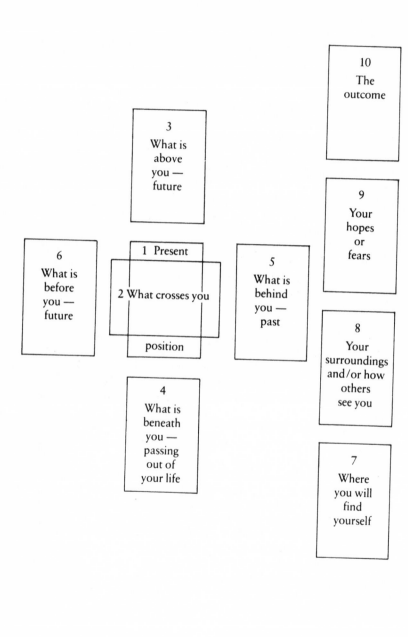

2. The Celtic Cross

Christopher

Christopher, a man of thirty-five years, married with twins, came for a reading regarding his unhappy marriage and his unsatisfactory work life. He was working as a solicitor in his uncle's firm, where he had been since leaving school, and Christopher felt very guilty about wanting to leave the family firm. He had married young, but his marriage had never been a happy one. Christopher really wanted to change direction in life, both personally and at work, and felt that he was under considerable internal pressure to do so.

Card one: King of Swords: present position

This card, in Chrisopher's present position, showed a strong figure of authority who is morally right and just, but with little compassion for individual problems. Christopher felt that this described his uncle perfectly and was afraid his uncle would not understand or forgive his wish to leave both job and marriage. Nevertheless, Christopher felt it was time he started living his own life and needed to grow up and away from his uncle's influence.

Card two: 8 of Pentacles: what crosses you

Crossing Christopher is the card of the apprentice, the card which indicates starting from the bottom and using skills and talents that might develop into a career. Christopher had always been interested in running his own restaurant and was pursuing the idea of taking a course in catering and starting up on his own. The card indicates that this is possible, but because it 'crosses' him, it will be difficult.

Card three, 3 of Cups: what is above you

This is the card of celebration and rejoicing in the future. Some solution or resolution is to be found and much happiness is to be experienced. However the 3's indicate initial completion and I warned Christopher that much work would need to be done after the first stage was reached.

Card four, 8 of Wands: what is beneath you

The 8 of Wands is a card of action and new direction, a time to be up and doing something, the end of delay and procrastination. Christopher told me he felt this kind of restlessness very much, and, as this placement indicates what is already present at the base of his life, it seemed an appropriate card to spur him on to action.

Card five, Knight of Pentacles: what is behind you

This card in the past position seemed, in Christopher's case, to represent his past action of plodding slowly, but surely, to a conclusion. He had been thinking of making a move for a very long time but could not quite find the courage to make a break, either career-wise or in his personal life, but with the Knight in the past it seemed to suggest that the process had finally reached a conclusion. He felt ready to take the plunge.

Card six, 7 of Wands: your immediate future

The 7 of Wands indicates stiff competition, but it also signified that, if Christopher could draw on his strength and determination to succeed, a satisfactory change of profession or career would follow. He was pleased by this card, saying he did not mind struggles or competition as long as it was in a field he had chosen himself.

Card seven, 4 of Wands: your future position

This card refers to how you find yourself in the future, how you feel about yourself, etc., and the card of 'harvest home' showed the possibility of Christopher reaping the benefit of what he worked hard to achieve. As the Wands represent creative ventures it could be that a new career would prove successful.

Card eight, 2 of Swords: your future environment

Christopher's future environment, represented by the 2 of Swords, seemed to suggest that, while his career or work-life may have been successfully changed, his personal life was still in a state of flux. The 2 of Swords shows the sense of indecision and stalemate, the figure depicted is steadfastly ignoring the rocks of hard fact and the sea of emotions. However, the appearance of this card indicated that the day of reckoning would soon be reached, and a decision made.

Card nine, 2 of Cups: your hopes and fears

The 2 of Cups is a card of reconciliation and unity. I asked Christopher how he felt about this card and he replied that he wanted, more than anything else, to be friends with his wife and to achieve an amicable relationship. The 2 of Cups often means a resolution of conflicts as well as the beginning of a new relationship. Christopher told me that, although he wanted to achieve a good relationship with his wife, he honestly did not think the marriage could continue. He wanted to be able to part friends and continue to remain on good terms with his wife and two boys.

Card ten, 8 of Cups: conclusion

This card shows a man turning his back on eight carefully stacked cups, heading towards barren mountains in the distance. It could suggest that Christopher would indeed leave behind all that he had worked so hard to achieve, disillusioned maybe, but possibly also able to face the reality of his situation.

3. The Star Spread

		7 The outcome — the top of the matter		

6
 Desires you have

5
 What is surfacing and soon to become known

4
 The heart of the matter

3
 Mind; thoughts; career

2
 Feelings; emotions; relationships

1
 Your present position — the root of the matter

I did a Major spread for Christopher and he chose the following cards.

Card one, Death: the root of the matter

The Death card, in Christopher's present position, indicates a time for change, transformation, endings and new beginnings. Both internally and externally, it seemed necessary for Christopher to let go of the old ways and values which were stifling and unproductive. Death indicated that the time was ripe to set this process in motion and, although it would be painful it would nevertheless provide a clear way to build a new life of his own.

Card two, The World: the emotions

The World is a very encouraging card to appear in the sphere of the feelings and emotions, for it indicates a goal is reached and a sense of wholeness achieved. Looking at card 5, the Hanged Man, it seems to suggest that if a sacrifice is made it will have a happy and beneficial outcome emotionally.

Card three, The Emperor: the intellect

Opposite the card for the feelings, which often describes relationships, the card for the intellect usually connects with things of a practical or rational nature, like work-life. The Emperor shows a solid influence which could mean that Christopher will find the strength of character to build a career for himself rather than relying on his family to support him. The Emperor, after all, teaches the Fool to be a man in his own right, so this may mean he will do the same for Christopher.

Card four, The Hermit: the heart of the matter

The centre of the spread is an important position, for the whole reading seems to revolve around it. The Hermit shows a need for inner contemplation and meditation, a time for patient self-examination. It is a time for withdrawal and thinking things through carefully. I suggested it might help for Christopher to seek some counselling to get a clearer picture of what was happening to him at this time, if he had trouble doing the inner meditation on his own.

Card five, The Hanged Man: the unconscious

In the place signifying the unconscious – that which is beneath the surface and about to emerge – is the Hanged Man. He indicates that a sacrifice must be made and that something must be given up in order to gain something of greater value. Christopher felt he understood this card quite well in that he knew a conscious decision would have to be taken by him alone. The essence of the Hanged Man is that the sacrifice is voluntary and made without outside pressure. Christopher had, to date, lived his life according to social dictates and now knew he would have to start making his own decisions.

Card Six, The Judgement: conscious desires

What is 'wanted consciously' is renewal, rebirth or rejuvenation. At last, it seems, Christopher's potential will have an opportunity to come to light, to be revealed and developed. The image of the dead rising and coffins opening to reveal talents hitherto unexplored, is an exciting one. After Death comes resurrection, and Judgement triumphantly indicates the new life and new opportunities. The Judgement is a 'Karmic' and so it suggests that rewards for past efforts will be reaped.

Card seven, The Lovers: the top of the matter

The Lovers end the spread with the hint of a relationship or marriage with a choice attached. The card might mean a new relationship altogether, or some choices made within the existing marriage. It is generally speaking a card of harmony, despite the element of choice or decision. Christopher will possibly have to choose between starting on a new love-affair or investigating further the potential of his marriage.

4. The Tree of Life

1 Spiritual	

3 Difficulty	**2** Responsibility
5 Opposing matters	**4** Helpful matters

6 Achievement

8 Communication and career	**7** Emotional relationships

9 Unconscious foundation

10 Home and family

Diana

Diana, a young woman in her mid-twenties, came for a reading when she was in the midst of changing her job, about to get married and move house. She was finding life understandably pressured and felt anxious to learn how these major decisions in her life would turn out. The reading unfolded as follows.

Card one, Ace of Pentacles: spiritual

The first card Diana drew was the Ace of Pentacles, in the position for spiritual matters. This card suggested that a new beginning with firm foundations was the framework for her spiritual life to grow in. It seemed she felt comfortable and happy with her inner beliefs and philosophies, and, because this card is usually connected with material wealth and turned up in the position for spiritual matters, it seemed to indicate that she was 'wealthy' in her spiritual life. Diana confirmed that firm spiritual beliefs lay at the base of her life and provided a good deal of comfort.

Card two, 2 of Wands: responsibility

The second card in the reading was the 2 of Wands, in the position of responsibility. This card hints at movement and change. It shows a merchant standing on the ramparts of his castle, looking out to sea and holding a globe. It suggests a longing to expand and grow, a longing to be getting on with life, and a move or change is indicated. Diana told me how much she wanted to get everything sorted out; her new home bought, her promotion at work settled and the wedding smoothly organized. She was anxious to progress from her present stable position, into a new life in terms of marriage and job, and was more than willing to undertake the extra responsibility.

Card three, 10 of Cups: difficulty

The 10 of Cups is a card illustrating ultimate happiness in family life. The picture of a happy couple watching their children playing, shows a life full of promise and joy. However, it is placed in a position of difficulty, so although it suggests these good things are available to Diana, it also indicates that they may prove more difficult to achieve than she anticipates. Her marriage will prove fruitful, but she will have to work at it. Diana admitted that she had not thought much about what would happen after the house move and marriage ceremony. I suggested that achieving and maintaining a satisfying marriage can be enormously hard work, but also enormously rewarding.

Card four, Justice: helpful matters

The calming, balancing influence of Justice, in this position, should prove extremely helpful in the midst of all the changing and rearranging Diana's life is going through. Justice is the card of logic and clear thinking, so it could help Diana work through her tasks steadily, and Justice's clarity of vision could help prevent things getting out of proportion.

Card five, Judgement: opposing matters

Judgement, the card of new life and rebirth, falling in opposing matters, shows that what is desired and appropriate, can also be problematic. Judgement shows the opening up of skills and talents which may be applied to her promotion at work, but this is an added pressure to her already full schedule. The new challenge offered by Judgement, shows that Diana's life is progressing positively, but she needs to remember that the period of stress that any change involves, has to be held together carefully. However, Justice is at hand to help bring this about.

Card six, 5 of Pentacles: achievement

The 5 of Pentacles, following the positive trend in the reading so far, is a card of warning regarding financial matters. The card shows two figures struggling through the snow, oblivious of the light from the window above them. They are unaware that help is at hand. Diana would do well to heed this warning which might be to do with not overstretching herself, either financially with the house purchase, or emotionally, which, she appreciated, she was in danger of doing. She told me she was under a lot of emotional pressure from her family and fiancé as well as workwise, and took the church window to represent the need to draw on her spiritual inner life for strength and support in the times of change.

Card seven, Knight of Swords: relationships

As the reading unfolded, alongside the encouraging aspects the earlier cards indicated, more factors began to emerge about her inner fears and worries. Firstly, the worry of the financial state of affairs represented by the 5 of Pentacles and then the Knight of Swords in the position of relationships. I asked whether the knight bore any similarity to her fiancé, but she said no. As we tried to place him in Diana's life she told me of an ex-boss who had also been quite a close friend and who portrayed similar character-istics to the Knight of Swords. Although Diana had not seen him for some time, he kept in touch and had phoned her unexpectedly a couple of days before the reading. She had told him excitedly about the latest developments in her life but got an uneasy feeling that he was not too pleased at the thought of her going off and getting married. He liked to think of her as single and available to have dinner with him occasionally. Diana was secretly afraid he might try and make trouble for her. She had been quite heavily influenced by him in the past and did not want him to alter her decisions by his disapproval.

Card eight, 10 of Wands: business

The warning trend set in motion by the previous few cards, seemed to continue in the next card, which covered her working life. The image on the card shows a figure overburdened by wands, carrying them rather awkwardly and with some difficulty. It seemed an appropriate message for Diana not to take on too much workwise, and to try and spread out her jobs in the easiest way possible. She told me she ought to delegate more at work, but hated not doing everything herself so was constantly getting caught in this way. The picture on the card helped clarify what she was doing to herself however, and she resolved to try to change that pattern.

Card nine, 8 of Cups: unconscious foundation

On an unconscious level, it seemed that Diana was not aware of how much was changing for her, and, while on the face of it the changes were good and desired ones, they also brought some stress and anxiety. All changes have repercussions but often, when they are wished for, people forget that they also provoke anxiety. The 8 of Cups shows Diana leaving behind the single life she had carefully built up and travelling towards the unknown fields of marriage. Diana felt that being able to acknowledge how scared she was of it, as well as happy about it, took some of the pressure off. She had felt afraid to admit her fear in case this meant she was doing the wrong thing.

Card ten, Ace of Cups: home life

The final card in Diana's reading is the Ace of Cups. The reading seems to have come full circle from one Ace to another. The card shows a home life which is happy and loving and suggests that, through all the difficulties Diana has to encounter, she will be able to experience major life moves and come to grips with them, resulting in a happy and emotionally satisfying relationship. The cards have mapped out the pitfalls to be avoided, the difficulties to be made conscious and finally indicate much love and happiness.

Further Examples

Emma

This is another example of a Celtic Cross reading done for Emma, aged twenty-five, who came to see me for advice on her career. She was working with computers and doing very well with extremely good prospects, but did not feel happy in a job which lacked close involvement with people. She was considering doing training in social work but was unsure if this would be the right move. Emotionally, she felt pretty low, as a long and important relationship had recently ended. Thus she was also interested in what was in store for her relationship-wise.

Card one, Page of Wands: present position

The card signifying her present position showed the beginnings of new creative activities and ideas with the possibility of opportunities arising. The page of Wands often indicates the opening up of new interests and pursuits, and, in Emma's case, seemed to suggest that she needed something new and stimulating in her career.

Card two, 10 of Swords: what crosses you

The card which crosses Emma is the 10 of Swords showing that something which has ended is still concerning her. Emma felt it was both the relationship ending, and her interest in her work waning, which was causing her to want to change direction. The 10 of Swords shows the end of something, graphically depicted by the man with the swords in his back, but the sun breaking over the water in the distance gives the message of new life. The ending of something in Emma's reading could be the relationship, but this card also carries the meaning that seeing something at its true value might result in disillusionment which could apply to her work. Emma had thought that her choice of career would result in a long-term commitment, but had become increasingly disappointed i n it.

Card three, 7 of Pentacles: difficulty

The 7 of Pentacles shows Emma trying to decide whether to continue with her established and successful work, symbolized by the pentacles hanging from the vine, or to turn to something new and untried, suggested by the single pentacle on the ground. A decision needs to be made but not rushed into.

Card four, 2 of Cups: what is above you

The card of harmony in relationships seemed to suggest that, although finished, Emma's relationship could remain amicable. It seemed a sense of harmony and understanding could be reached so that a true friendship could emerge out of the existing relationship. The 2 of Cups can suggest reconciliation as well as firm friendship.

Card five, 3 of Wands: what is behind you

This card symbolizes her past efforts in working steadily at her career towards a certain level, thinking that when she reached it she would be satisfied. Emma had just reached this level only to discover that her horizons had expanded and that there were now other things interesting her which she had previously not considered.

Card six, Page of Swords: your immediate future

This card in the immediate future indicates gossip or back-biting as the Page of Swords can indicate a person who spreads unpleas-

ant stories or rumours. I cautioned Emma not to pay any attention
if such gossip came to her attention because, as a page is a 'small'
card, nothing much will grow from it unless it is fostered.

Card seven, Queen of Wands: your future position

The card signifying Emma's future position is the Queen of
Wands 'queen of hearth and home', an active, energetic woman
who has both family and work well in hand. Emma indicated that
she would like a husband and family at some point, but also felt
that she would want to keep her own interests alive. The Queen of
Wands suggested that she could have both.

Card eight, Page of Cups: your future environment

The third Page in Emma's spread showed that a great many things
seemed to be budding and new possibilities were opening on a
number of fronts. The Page of Cups suggests that new feelings
would emerge and hurt feelings would heal, so she could love and
trust again. This card also indicates the birth of something,
whether it be a child, a relationship or new creative feelings.

Card nine, 2 of Swords: your hopes and fears

This card in the slot for Emma's hopes or fears showed that she
was afraid she would remain indecisive, unable to make a move.
She was concerned that she was doomed to her current situation
of stalemate, neither happy nor desperately sad, but this card
indicates that once the problem is brought to light or to consciousness, it can be faced and then dealt with.

Card ten, 8 of Cups: conclusion

The fears surrounding the 2 of Swords seemed unfounded, as the
final card of the reading, the 8 of Cups, shows a figure walking
away from a carefully constructed situation, towards the barren

hills in search of something new. It seemed that Emma would indeed find the motivation and/or courage to change her direction in due course. As there were so many pages or 'small beginnings' in the spread it seemed that it would be a while before Emma made concrete what she really wanted and that she should take plenty of time in deciding because once she made the decision it would be final.

THE STAR SPREAD

The Major Arcana reading for Emma went as follows:

Card one, The High Priestess: the root of the matter

At the root of the matter, the High Priestess reveals potential unfilfilled and uncharted terrain waiting to be discovered. This card suggested that the time was ripe for Emma to draw back the veil of the unconscious to reveal her hidden wishes and talents. The High Priestess is a card symbolizing feminine intuition as well as secret wishes and dreams becoming known, so it seemed an appropriate card to start this spread. The High Priestess suggests interest and search for knowledge of a complex and deep nature, especially connected with the unconscious mind, so the high-powered, logic-oriented world of computers did not fit too well with the new turn in Emma's inner growth process.

Card two, The Fool: the emotions

The Fool appeared in the slot for relationships and feelings which seemed to indicate the necessity for taking a risk, jumping off the edge of an emotional precipice. In Emma's case, I felt it heralded a new relationship coming into play. She would have to let go of her fears and self-protective instincts and take the plunge. She was understandably nervous about getting involved again but the Fool's presence would fill her with enthusiasm and adventure, thus encouraging her to overcome this fear.

Card three, Temperance: the intellect

The position for work-life was dominated by Temperance, a gentle card, showing a time for compassion and cooperation to come into her career. Emma's interest and inclination towards social work, in which she could use her skills in helping others, seemed to match Temperance's appearance in the reading. It seemed, at any rate, that her working life would be more harmonious and congenial.

Card four, The Lovers: the heart of the matter

The heart of the matter seemed to confirm the indications the cards held for the start of a new relationship as the Lovers combined with the Fool to suggest that the time would soon be ripe for Emma to start a new love affair. The Lovers has the added message of 'trial or choice' which indicates that a conscious decision will have to be taken in order for Emma to get involved emotionally or to make a deep commitment.

Card five, The Wheel of Fortune: the unconscious

The Wheel of Fortune in the position of the unconscious, shows that a new chapter is about to start in Emma's life. As the Wheel turns, she will have a new opportunity to take more responsibility for her life and to make positive future plans. The Wheel of Fortune often brings good luck as well as marking the commencement of a new cycle. 'The old order changeth.'

Card six, The Moon: conscious desires

The shifting, moving influence of the Moon shows uncertainty and mood swings connected with Emma's conscious desires. I suggested that the more she became aware of what was beneath the surface within her, as symbolized by the crayfish crawling out of the pool, the easier it would be for her to make up her mind on a course of action. The Moon often signifies a time when dreams and intuitions should be focused on and pure logical or rational thought should take a back seat. I felt, intuitively, that the direction and course of action would slowly emerge, rather than strike suddenly and unmistakably like lightning.

Card seven, Judgement: the top of the matter

This message of rebirth and renewal, as a concluding card, shows that a cycle will be completed and rewards reaped from seeds of past effort. At the appropriate time, Emma's unrevealed and unfulfilled potential will be opened up and made conscious, as hinted at by the High Priestess at the root of the matter. If Emma gave herself sufficient time to allow the energies of the cards to unfold gradually, she would be sure of which direction to take and a positive new life would follow.

Conclusion

Now that you have studied all the examples, the last exercise is to put all you have learned so far into practice. It is time to experiment and to try readings for your friends, family and yourself, as you now begin to develop your own style and method. It is a good idea to continue using the 'guided fantasy' exercise to improve and enrich your understanding of the Tarot images, but, at this stage in your journey, the experiments and experiences of the moment will enable you to start interpreting readings at the various levels from which the Tarot can be approached. This will ultimately prove the most rewarding and satisfying aspect of the study.

So now, in true Tarot fashion, we find we have come full circle. Just as the World symbolizes both the completion of a cycle and the foetus ready to be born again as the Fool, so you are starting out again, this time discovering the Tarot for yourself. I do hope your adventures will be as exciting and interesting as mine were and still are.

Bibliography

Cavendish, Richard, *The Tarot* (Michael Joseph, London, 1975)

Douglas, Alfred, *The Tarot* (Penguin, London, 1973)

Graves, Robert, *The White Goddess* (Vintage Books, New York, 1958)

Gray, Eden, *The Tarot Revealed* (Inspiration House, New York, 1958)

Huson, Paul, *The Devil's Picturebook* (Abacus, London, 1971)

Pollack, Rachel, *Seventy-eight Degrees of Wisdom* (The Aquarian Press, Northamptonshire, 1983)

Waite, A.E. *The Pictorial Key to the Tarot* (First pub. 1910 Rider, London, 1971)

Yates, Frances, *The Art of Memory* (Routledge & Kegan Paul, London, 1966)